THE LITTLE BOOK OF
FLIGHT

Written by David Curnock

THE LITTLE BOOK OF
FLIGHT

This edition first published in the UK in 2006
By Green Umbrella Publishing

© Green Umbrella Publishing 2007

www.greenumbrella.co.uk

Publishers Jules Gammond and Vanessa Gardner

Printed and bound in China

ISBN 978-1-905009-33-6

Contents

Chapter 1

Myths and Legends

"Man must rise above the Earth – to the top of the atmosphere and beyond – for only thus will he fully understand the world in which he lives."

– Socrates

THE HISTORY OF HUMAN FLIGHT may be much older than we could ever have dared to imagine. Some believe there is evidence that hints at the existence of manned flight thousands of years ago. While these beliefs have not been proven, it is undeniable that mankind has long had the desire to emulate the birds and take to the skies. Many ancient legends tell of attempts to fly using bird-like wings, fashioned from wood and feathers or cloth, strapped to the limbs of the would-be flyer.

descriptions of the view that unfolds before them.

The eagle said to him, to Etana:

"My friend, the *[missing word]* are obvious,
Come, let me take you up to heaven,
Put your chest against my chest,
Put your hands against my wing feathers,
Put your arms against my sides".

He put his chest against his chest,
He put his hands against his wing feathers,
He put his arms against his sides,
Great indeed was the burden upon him.
When he bore him aloft one league,

The eagle said to him, to Etana:

"Look, my friend, how the land is now,
Examine the sea, look for its boundaries,
The land is hills...
The sea has become a stream".

Ancient Babylon

THE EARLIEST RECORDED REFERence to aviation appears within a set of Babylonian laws dating from around 2400 BC, the Halkatha:

"To operate a flying machine is a great privilege. Knowledge of flying is most ancient, a gift of the gods of old for saving lives."

Other Babylonian scripts are purported to refer to the magical flight of Etana, on the back of an enormous eagle. The eagle takes him higher and higher, and throughout the narrative there are remarkably authentic

The Orientals

ANCIENT CHINESE TEXTS CONTAIN numerous references to experiments with flying machines. Some of these texts have been dated prior to the year 2000 BC. Legends variously tell of emperors flying with wings, and in chariots. Around the period 2200 BC, the Emperor Shun reportedly used two large reed hats to escape from a burning tower, and then fly to safety over his domain. This was, almost certainly, the first historical reference to parachuting. Similar feats were to be told in the mythology of almost every civilisation in the ancient world.

In 1766 BC the Emperor Cheng Tang is believed to have ordered the construction of a flying machine that was subsequently destroyed in order that '...none should discover the secret of flight.' In the 3rd century BC, the Chinese poet Chu Yun claimed to have made a detailed aerial survey of the Gobi desert, giving special praise to the durability of his craft to withstand winds and sand storms. Around 400 BC the Chinese discovered how to make, and fly, kites. Used by the Chinese in religious ceremonies,

RIGHT Kite flying In Beijing. Kites date back to more than 2,000 years ago, when they were made in China from bamboo and silk

they were also built for fun, as well as for more practical reasons, including their use in weather observations. The invention of the kite was significant, as mankind began to study the effect of wind and weather on the behaviour and control of flying machines.

The Chinese are also credited with the invention of the rocket: this development was, almost certainly, a spin-off from the manufacture of fireworks in the centuries BC. An ancient drawing of a rocket-powered chair, fitted with two kites to provide lift, purports to show the Chinese Emperor Wan-Ho about to take to the skies: the success or failure of his mission was not documented. The first recorded use of the rocket is dated to the year 1232 AD, when the invading Mongols used arrows propelled by rockets as they laid siege

BELOW Emperor Wan-Ho and his Rocket Chair

RIGHT Icarus plunging into the sea after the sun melted his wings. Daedalus flew on homeward

to the city of Kaifeng. Transcripts of ancient legends from Nepal also mention powered flight. These state that only the people known as the Yavanas knew the real secrets of flight. The reference to the Yavanas can be interpreted as pertaining to the light-skinned people of the eastern Mediterranean, particularly Greece. This is highly significant because Greece is the origin of one of the best known mythical accounts of the perils associated with early aviation.

Ancient Greece

THE STORY OF DAEDALUS AND Icarus is perhaps the most widely known of the ancient aviation myths. The poet Ovid described Daedalus as a highly skilled architect, the designer of the maze, or labyrinth, at Knossus on the island of Crete. By the time this task was completed he had become homesick, but Daedalus knew that King Minos would prevent him from returning to his homeland across the sea. Therefore, Daedalus decided to build a flying machine. Ovid reported him as saying: " The king may block my way by land or across the ocean, but the sky, surely, is open, and that is how we shall go." According to Ovid: "With these words, he set his mind to sciences never explored before, and altered the laws of nature."

Daedalus prepared two flying craft, one for himself and the other for his son Icarus. The craft were constructed from local materials, including feathers held together with wax. Daedalus became the earliest recorded flying instructor as he briefed his son on the principles of flight prior to their departure. He instructed his son to fly at a middle altitude: high enough to prevent the spray from the sea from dampening the wings, and thus make them too heavy, and low enough so that the heat of the sun would not melt the wax that held the feathers together. The two aviators then headed homeward, away from Crete, across the Aegean Sea. Icarus, intoxicated by the thrill of flying, forgot his father's instructions and flew too close to the sun. This caused the wax of the wings to melt, and he was lost in the deep blue waters. Other legends from the Grecian and Macedonian empires tell how Alexander the Great was reported to have "...harnessed four Griffins to a basket, and flew around his realm."

Persia

AROUND THE PERIOD 1500 BC, the Persian King Kai Kawus was "...tempted by evil spirits to invade heaven with the help of a flying craft. This craft consisted of a throne, to the corners of which were attached four long poles pointing upward. Pieces of meat were placed at the top of each pole and ravenous eagles were chained to the feet. As the eagles attempted to fly

upward to the meat, they carried the throne aloft. In flight, somewhere over China, the eagles tired and the throne came crashing down, resulting in the death of the intrepid aviator. Known subsequently as "The Foolish King", his exploits were recounted, in 1000 AD, by the poet Ferdowski in his Book of Kings.

ABOVE Daedalus and Icarus, a portrait by Charles Paul Landon, 1799

Egypt

IN 1898 AN ANCIENT ARTEFACT was discovered in a tomb near Saqqara. This item was, at the time, thought to be a model of a bird, and was catalogued as such. Subsequent research led to the conclusion that the object resembled a modern aircraft. Further examination by experts in aerodynamics concluded that the model was remarkably airworthy, "…indicating knowledge of principles of aircraft design which had taken European and American designers a century of airfoil experimental work to discover." Other authorities held the view that it was, as originally believed, just a stylised model of a bird.

At the 3,000-year old temple of Seti the First, located several hundred miles south of Cairo and the Giza Plateau at Abydos, a stone roof beam just inside the entrance bears some intriguing images. One of these appears to be a helicopter, together with an aircraft or spaceship, amongst others. Some experts claim these images are proof that flying machines could have existed all those years ago. Claims that the images are UFOs have also been made, while some Egyptologists believe they are hoaxes.

RIGHT Hieroglyphics in the tomb of King Pepi I at Saqqara, Egypt. Second row from left, fourth item down shows what could be interpreted as an 'aeroplane-like' image

South America

THOUGHT TO COME FROM A PRE-Inca culture a so called 'Gold Jet', measuring two inches long and shaped like a modern fighter plane, was discovered in Colombia. Aviation experts noted that the shape of the wings, and the tapering of the fuselage, implied that the original aircraft was jet powered and capable of supersonic speeds. As in the case of the Egyptian finds, sceptics pointed out that the object could just as easily represent a bird or flying fish. However, a study of the tail of the object, in particular the triangular upright tailfin that carried an insignia resembling that on a modern warplane, concluded that it bore little similarity to either bird or fish.

India

IN INDIA, AN ANCIENT COLLECTION of sacred Hindu books, the Samaranga Sutradhara, contains at least 200 stanzas concerning almost every aspect of flying. A special study into these works came to the conclusion that they contained a great knowledge of aviation, including that of flying machines and equipment, remarkably similar to those we know today. These texts refer to the flying machines as Vimanas. They possessed "...carefully welded joints", and were heated and driven "...by controlled fire from the iron containers...", thus bearing some similarity to modern jet powered planes, even down to the noise that they made. The noise was described as being like "...the roar of a lion", and setting the machine in motion so that "...the traveller sitting inside the Vimana may travel in the air, to such a distance as to look like a pearl in the sky."

RIGHT Man-powered
aircraft the Gossamer
Albatross crossed
the English Channel
in 1979

Polynesia

IN THE SOUTH PACIFIC ISLANDS of Polynesia there are again more references to early flight. Here local legends talk of a fair skinned people who arrived from the west aboard "shining boats", that "flew above the sea." Other island groups of the Pacific have similar legends of "flying canoes" that brought with them people from afar.

Europe

IN 863 BC, THE CELTIC RULER KING Bladud came to the British throne. He travelled to Greece, where he created huge wings made of chicken feathers, and flew over the city of New Troy. However, he lost control and crashed into the Temple of Apollo, where he died on impact, having ruled Britain for twenty years.

According to both British and Germanic legend, there is a tale of how one known as Wayland the Smith was '…carried into the sky by a shirt made of feathers.' Wayland and his two brothers were imprisoned on an island in Sweden. Wayland asked one of his brothers, Egil, to fashion him a pair of wings, which would enable him to escape. Having first caught some wild birds, Egil used their feathers to construct the wings. After collecting his wings, Wayland flew into the sky and eventually came to rest across the North Sea in Britain. He landed on the high downs in Berkshire, where he discovered an ancient chambered tomb in which he made his home. It was here that the legendary Merlin commissioned him to make the mighty sword Excalibur for King Arthur.

Africa

THE AFRICAN CONTINENT ALSO had legends telling of human flight. In Uganda there was once a powerful king, within whose army the flying warrior Kibaga was employed on reconnaissance missions to seek out the positions of their enemies. The king then attacked with his army and was supported by Kibaga, who flew over the enemy and dropped large pieces of rock onto them, killing many.

Chapter 2

Early Designs and Glorious Failures

"A bird is an instrument working according to mathematical law, which instrument it is within the capacity of man to reproduce with all its movements."

– Leonardo da Vinci, 1505

THE CONCEPT THAT BIRDS SEEM to fly with very little effort led many along the path toward the idea that, in order for man to fly, it was necessary for him to emulate birds. Ancient myths about flight had involved fashioning wings out of birds' feathers. Many would-be aviators sought to achieve flight by similar means, often with dire consequences. Since ancient times there were others who believed that the mechanics of bird flight was more complex than it first appeared. The history of the early centuries of the first millennium AD showed some instances of thoughtful and, in some cases, scientific reasoning being applied to the problems to be overcome before man could eventually achieve flight. Others took a more practical but somewhat foolhardy approach, in order to take to the air, as related in the story of the flying monk.

Elmer: the Flying Monk of Malmesbury

IN BRITAIN IN THE YEAR 1010 AD, a monk named Elmer (sometimes spelt 'Eilmer', and also known as Oliver) of Malmesbury Abbey in Wiltshire, became the first successful tower jumper. Previous attempts, by others, to fly by jumping off high places with a contraption of wings attached to the arms or body of the would-be flyer, had usually ended in the death of the jumper. Elmer decided to attempt to emulate the flight of Daedalus by constructing a set of wings, and using them to fly from the top of the abbey tower. The framework of the wings was fashioned from wood and covered with a thin cloth or parchment stretched over the frame. The wings were then attached to his arms and feet. The story of Elmer's flight, as recounted by the historian William of Malmesbury in the following century, tells of a downward glide of about 250 yards, ending with a crash-landing in which Elmer broke both legs. The crash was probably due to air turbulence around the tower, coupled with an inherent lack of stability of his machine. William's report of the event, as recounted to him by monks who knew Elmer in his later years, stated: "What with the violence of the wind and the eddies, and at the same time his consciousness of the temerity of the attempt, he faltered and fell, breaking

ABOVE Elmer the Flying Monk. Dedicated window in Malmesbury Abbey showing Elmer holding a model of his wings

and crippling both his legs." A short-coming in the design of the wings, also chronicled by the historian William, told of Elmer's admitted lack of foresight in that "…he forgot to fit a tail on his hinder parts."

Roger Bacon

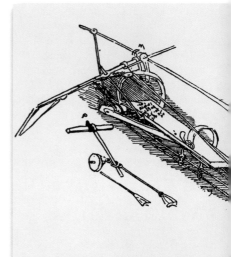

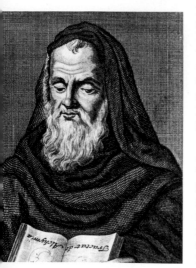

SOME TWO HUNDRED YEARS after Elmer there lived a man who, to this day, is considered by many to have possessed one of the greatest minds of all time. He was also the first to write, in a studied and scientific manner, about the possibility of human flight. Roger Bacon was a Franciscan monk who lived in England from 1214 AD to 1292 AD. A prolific writer, Bacon vigorously promoted the power of reason, and poured scorn on the ignorance and misinformation that existed throughout the so-called Dark Ages. In 1260, Bacon wrote a work on the subject, in which he stated: "…human reason is so powerful that it could even manage to do something that seems utterly impossible, namely, build a machine that would enable a person to fly." The manuscript, published some three hundred years later, outlines two of the ways that Bacon considered a human might fly. The first is a description, albeit a rough one, of a device which utilised the 'flapping wing' principle and later became known as the ornithopter. The other is a

Leonardo Da Vinci

THE PERIOD BETWEEN ABOUT 1485 AD to 1900 AD was notable for the increasing number of those who designed flying machines. Some of the designs were born more out of hope than science and, therefore, could only be classed as abject failures. To modern eyes, many of these machines appear to be totally unsuited to the purpose of flight but were, at the time, believed to be viable as a means to achieve manned flight. There were also those who carried out their design work and research into flight in a great deal of secrecy, a necessary precaution in times when such work could have been considered as witchcraft or sorcery.

One of the more secretive of these designers lived in Florence, Italy, in the late fifteenth century. The great artist and scientist Leonardo da Vinci, whose work in the field of aviation remained virtually unknown until published in the late nineteenth century, told few except the most trusted of his contemporaries about his aeronautical writings

LEFT Ornithopter sketches by Leonardo Da Vinci, circa 1500 AD

more detailed description, with scientific justification of his theory, for a balloon described as being a globe filled with 'ethereal air'. Bacon was of the opinion that air is a fluid in which less dense objects might float, much as a ship floats in water. He even outlined the methods for thinning the air contained within the globe, thus giving it the buoyancy necessary for it to rise into the air: all this happened around five hundred years before the reality of the lighter than air balloon.

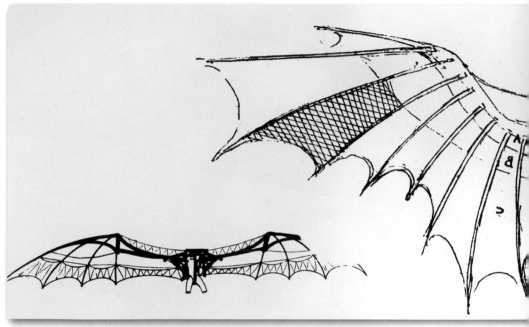

ABOVE Sketches of Glider by Leonardo Da Vinci

and sketches. He even took the precaution of using the technique of reversed 'mirror' writing to conceal his theories from prying eyes.

Many of Leonardo's designs were based on the wings of birds and bats, his legacy of more than five hundred sketches, and thirty-five thousand words, bearing testament to his work.

He was astute enough to realise that the human body was not capable of bird-like flight yet, paradoxically, he produced designs for many ornithopter flying machines that would each have required the aviator to pedal with the feet, and flap with the arms, to propel the machine. Since his assumptions on how birds fly were subsequently proved

incorrect, manned flight with this type of craft would have been virtually impossible.

Leonardo's findings, however, were not all based on incorrect assumptions. He was aware of the need for an aircraft to have a tail section to stabilise the machine in flight, this requirement remaining valid until more recent times when, largely due to new materials and better design technology, some tail-less 'flying wing' aircraft took to the skies. He also pre-dated the helicopter, as we know it today, with a design sketch for an aircraft that utilised a large tapered screw to bore through the air, and lift the aircraft vertically into flight. The major flaw in this concept was that the motive power was again to be provided by a human being. Da Vinci apparently made only one model of any of his designs, that being a miniature

version of his helicopter. He noted that his machine would have to wait until there was a source of power lighter than a human, for it to work. It was not until the twentieth century that the dream of bird-like flight was eventually realised. In 1942 Adalbert Schmid made the first successful manned ornithopter flight, of around fifteen minutes, at Munich Leim, Germany. However, his ornithopter was powered by an internal combustion engine, rather than the pilot's own muscles.

BELOW Helicopter by Leonardo Da Vinci, 1483

RIGHT Besnier's
flapping paddle
wings,1678

Besnier

IN THE PERIOD LEADING UP TO
the beginning of the nineteenth century
there had been, according to the historian Clive Hart in his book 'The
Prehistory of Flight', more than fifty
documented instances of attempts at
manned flight. Of these, there were
probably around only twelve that could
be considered as legitimate, achieving
somewhat brief periods of flight, or gliding. One of the first humans to attempt
flight, with a mechanical device, was a
locksmith named Besnier from Sable, in
France. In 1678, he created a simple,
glider-type flying machine consisting of
a pair of wood-and-taffeta wings worn
on the back, and two rods pivoted on his
shoulders. At the ends of each rod were
small V-shaped planes, these being controlled by the hands and feet for the purposes of either gliding or, to provide
flight propulsion. Besnier is said to have
launched himself from the roof of his
home, flying over a barn, before landing
on another roof. While there was always
some doubt about Besnier's claims,
those who believed them to be true were
inspired to experiment further.

Theories Abound

MANY FLIGHT ATTEMPTS MET
with failure as the potential aeronauts
crashed, usually with fatal consequences. After many disastrous
attempts to "fly like a bird" it was apparent that there was a great deal of fresh
thinking to be applied to the subject
before flight could be achieved. During
the seventeenth and eighteenth centuries, there were several scientific findings that led to the greater
understanding of the properties of air,
including the way it acts to exert forces
in a particular manner, under certain
conditions. The development of the

propeller owes much to the study of windmills and waterwheels by John Smeaton, and others, during the eighteenth century.

The principle of adapting Archimedes' theory on buoyancy, using an object that was lighter than the air it displaced, was written in a paper produced in Brescia, Italy, in the year 1670 by a priest, Father Francesco de Lana. In his treatise, De Lana suggested that, by creating a sphere using thin sheets of copper, and evacuating the sphere of all air, such an object would be lighter than the air it displaced and thus, would rise into the air. Although his theory was sound, the practical difficulties of manufacturing sufficiently light spheres, that would

not collapse under the pressure of the surrounding air, proved too difficult. In 1766, the British scientist Henry Cavendish discovered hydrogen gas, which was calculated to be one-tenth the weight of air. The possibility that hydrogen gas could be used to fill a balloon, and thus make it lighter than air, was not grasped at the time: therefore, the first balloons to fly were filled with hot air.

One of the more bizarre ideas was the flying boat of Barthelmy-Laurent de Gusman, from 1709, whereby the craft was to be kept aloft by magnets in two globes, placed fore and aft. There is no scientific evidence to support the reasoning behind his theory.

Francois Blanchard

AROUND THE YEAR 1781 A FRENCH inventor, Francois Blanchard, designed and built a flying machine based on the ornithopter principle, and known as the 'Vaisseau Volant' (Flying Vessel). According to a description of the machine in the 'Journal de Paris', ".... it had four great wings that were attached to a light car. The operator sat inside, controlling the wings with his hand and foot pedals and levers." Unfortunately, Blanchard failed to leave the ground but had demonstrated his understanding of the requirement for a system of controls. Blanchard later became a respected figure in the science of aerodynamics, as well as one of the great ballooning pioneers.

Emanuel Swedenborg

A FURTHER TWO HUNDRED years elapsed before the next significant design for an aircraft was revealed. In 1715, Emanuel Swedenborg a Swedish scientist, inventor, theologian and philosopher, designed a 'Machine for Flying', the so-called Daedalian. This was a remarkably well thought-out design that featured a wheeled landing gear, a curve-formed lifting surface, a centrally located position for the aviator, and beating blades for propulsion. These blades could also be manipulated to provide some means of control in

flight. The Swedenborg design was a major departure from the 'flapping wing' ornithopter, in that it utilised the principle of air flowing over a curved surface, in order to generate lift.

Henson and Stringfellow

AMONG THOSE ENGINEERS FAMiliar with the work of Sir George Cayley (see Chapter 3), was an engineer and inventor named William Samuel Henson who, together with his associate John Stringfellow, produced a design for a large steam-powered, passenger carrying monoplane. The 'Henson Aerial Steam Carriage' was patented in 1842, and had a wingspan of around 150 feet. In the following year, Henson demonstrated his design using a small-scale model, which may have achieved a short flight while fixed to a guide wire. However, subsequent attempts to fly a larger model met with failure.

Although his attempts to fly his steam carriage failed, much of Henson's design work had great merit, and set a precedent for aeronautical designers

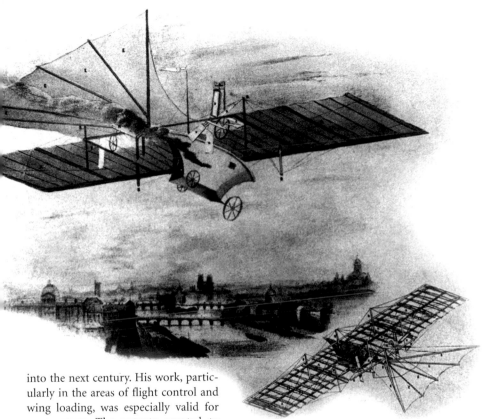

into the next century. His work, particularly in the areas of flight control and wing loading, was especially valid for many years. The patents granted to Henson for his monoplane included those for "…rectangular shaped wings with curved upper and lower surfaces, the wings being constructed from a series of wooden ribs attached to tapering tubular spars, all covered with fabric, and braced with internal and external wires." With its tricycle landing gear and contra-rotating propellers, the comparatively modern-looking Henson monoplane design, albeit with a bird-like tail, had most of the attributes of a true 'flying machine', rather than those of a bird.

Chapter 3

Man Begins to Fly

"To invent an airplane is nothing. To build one is something. To fly is everything."
– Otto Lilienthal

MANY HAVE ASPIRED TO ACHIEVE all three of the tenets stated by Lilienthal; to invent, build and then fly, a machine of their own. Some chose the balloon; many attempted to emulate the flight of birds by flapping, or gliding, with bird-like wings. Although the arrival of powered flight, as we know it today, was around a hundred years into the future, there were many who applied new vigour to the search for flight. They were often inspired by the attempts of others whose work they had seen at first hand, or read about in the scientific journals of the time.

The Montgolfier Brothers

THE MONTGOLFIER BROTHERS Joseph, born in 1740, and Étienne, who was born five years later, were from a family of sixteen children. Their father owned a paper manufacturing company at Viladon-les-Annonay, near Lyon, France. Both brothers were fascinated

RIGHT The Montgolfier brothers carry out their first experiment with an unmanned hot-air balloon at Annonay

by the idea of floating in the air, like the clouds, and looking down on the world below.

One of Joseph's early experiments had involved obtaining some paper from the factory, making a large bag, and filling it with steam, in the hope that the device would rise into the air. The end result was failure, and a sodden mass of paper. His brother Étienne had read many scientific papers that gave him the idea of making a bag float in the air, the bag being filled with hydrogen gas, obtained from sulphuric acid and iron filings, but again without success. Further experiments took place indoors during November 1782, with Joseph achieving some measure of success using a taffeta envelope, filled with hot air, which rose to the ceiling. The brothers were spurred by this reward and, with an envelope made from segments of taffeta that were joined by buttons, and lined with paper fireproofed with alum, they optimistically prepared a large-scale experimental balloon.

Joseph and Étienne saw their hopes and dreams become reality with their first public demonstration on June 4th 1783, when their hot air balloon took off from a site near their home at

Premier Voyage Aérien. Experience faite à Sous la Direction Par M.^r le Marquis d'Arlandes En présence de M.^r le Dauphin, dans le Jardin de la Muette, de Mr Montgolfier, et Mr Pilâtre du Rosier, le 21 9.bre 1783

Annonay. With a volume of around eight hundred cubic metres, the balloon reached a height of around a thousand metres, and covered a distance of two kilometres. They were successful, even though they failed to fully understand the physics involved, believing that it was smoke that provided the lift, the balloon being filled with smoke generated from a fire of straw, wool, and even some old shoe leather. They believed that the denser the smoke, the greater the lift would be. Only later was it discovered that it was hot air from the fire that created the lift, and not the smoke.

Their second recorded flying demonstration took place in Paris, in the presence of King Louis XVI, on September 19th 1783, for which they built a new balloon with a volume of some fourteen hundred cubic metres. This flight was notable in that the balloon carried three passengers; namely a duck, a cock and a sheep, in order to test the effects of altitude on live creatures. The successful flight landed three kilometres away, having reached a height of five hundred metres.

On November 21st 1783, the Montgolfier brothers finally achieved their goal, using an even larger balloon with a volume of twenty-two thousand

Francois Blanchard

INSPIRED BY HOT-AIR-BALLOON flights demonstrated by his compatriots the Montgolfier brothers, Francois Blanchard turned to the balloon as his means of becoming airborne and, on March 2nd 1784, made his first successful ascent in a self-built balloon. On January 7th 1785, Blanchard and Dr. John Jeffries, an American physician, made the first flight across the English Channel from Dover, England, to Calais, France. In the same year, Blanchard gave a successful demonstration of the use of a parachute, when a basket containing a small animal was dropped from a balloon, and then parachuted to earth. On January 9th 1793, Blanchard made the first balloon flight by a human in North America, when he ascended from the Washington Prison Yard in Philadelphia, Pennsylvania, and landed in Gloucester County, New Jersey. Carrying the first airmail letter, this flight was observed by President George Washington. In addition to his balloon flights in France and North

cubic metres, and with hot air provided by an iron furnace. Two men, Jean-François Pilâtre, a French physicist, and François Laurent, the Marquis d'Arlandes, became the first humans to achieve an untethered flight in a lighter-than-air device. They reached a height of nine hundred metres, and landed ten kilometres away, some twenty-five minutes later. Amazingly, the Montgolfier brothers had achieved their ambitions within a remarkably short period of time, the entire project taking just one year from concept to its successful outcome.

OPPOSITE LEFT
The first untethered manned ascent of the Montgolfier hot-air balloon carrying Pilatre and the Marquis d'Arlandes, 1783

LEFT Inventors of the hot air balloon, Joesph and Etienne Montgolfier

America, Blanchard also made the first balloon flights in Germany, Belgium, Poland, and the Netherlands. Unfortunately, in February 1808, Blanchard suffered a heart attack while on a flight over The Hague in the Netherlands, and fell more than 50 feet. He never recovered from the fall and died, the following year, on March 7th 1809.

Sir George Cayley

TOWARD THE END OF the eighteenth century one of the great names in the history of aviation, Sir George Cayley, made his first flying machine, a model helicopter with contra-rotating propellers. Cayley was probably the first to have fully understood the principles of flight, together with the knowledge of the forces acting on the machine. In 1799, Cayley inscribed a silver medallion with an image of the forces that apply in flight: on the reverse side, he sketched his design for a monoplane glider. In 1804, Cayley designed and built a model mono-plane glider that fea-tured a movable cruciform tail, a kite-shaped wing with a high angle of inci-dence, and a moveable weight to alter the centre of gravity. This glider was probably the first gliding device to make a significant number of flights. Using various models to aid his research, he soon discovered that wings with dihedral, those with their outer end set higher than their inner end, vastly improved the lateral stability of the machine. By 1807 he had learned that, for a given surface area, a wing with an upward curve to its top surface provided more 'lift' than one with a flat surface.

Sir George published a remarkable paper titled "On Aerial Navigation" in 1810. This essay outlined the three basic requirements for successful flight as being, lift, propulsion, and control. He was also active in the development of

ing machine flew on at least one occasion, albeit a very short flight. A few years later in 1853, Sir George built an even larger gliding machine, and had his coachman on-board for the first flight. It was later reported that the coachman was not enamoured with the situation, and had stated that he was employed to drive a coach, not to fly a gliding machine!

Sir George Cayley was of the opinion that a powerful, but light, 'prime-mover' was needed before powered flight could be achieved. Unfortunately, his several attempts at building internal combustion engines fuelled with gunpowder grains were not successful, mainly on the grounds of unreliability. However, Cayley's activities in the field of aeronautics have since been recognised as being those of the single, most important aeronautical theoretician and designer of his era, and a great inspiration for those who followed.

lighter-than-air flying machines and designed a semi-rigid airship. He had the notion that the use of several separate gasbags, within the airship, would be an added safety feature, thus limiting the loss of gas, and therefore lift, in the event of damage.

In 1849, Cayley built a large gliding machine, similar to the 1799 design inscribed on the silver medallion, and tested the device with a 10-year old boy aboard. It was reported that the glid-

Horatio Phillips

HORATIO FREDERICK PHILLIPS, the son of a gunsmith, was born in 1845 in Streatham, London. From an early age he was enthralled by the study of aeronautics, in particular the design and testing of aerofoils, in which field he made what was later to be seen as a major contribution to the future development of aircraft. In 1884, Phillips tested a variety of aerofoil sections in a new design of wind tunnel that used a steam injector to suck air in through the entrance of the tunnel. Phillips was granted patents for his double-curvature aerofoil wing sections. His 1884 patent described how the air passed over his wing "… in such a way as to as to cause a partial vacuum to be created over a portion of the upper surface of the blade thus aiding the air below to support the weight."

In 1893, he constructed a large device for testing the effective lift of what he termed "sustainers". This device, known as the 'Phillips Flying Machine', was over nine feet tall, about 22 feet in length, and had 40 lifting surfaces. Driven by a two-bladed propeller powered by a steam engine, the machine was tethered to a frame mounted on a circular track of some 200 feet in diameter. The machine lifted a total weight of 402 pounds, to a height of some three feet, at a speed of about 40 miles per hour. Phillips continued to experiment with the use of multiple lifting surfaces, and produced some rather bizarre designs in order to demonstrate that his theories were sound. In the same year, he produced a flying machine with 50 lifting surfaces that resembled a giant venetian blind, and was powered by a propeller driven by a coal-fired engine. This tethered machine again rose some three feet above a larger 628 feet diameter test track, and reached a speed of around 40 miles per hour, becoming airborne for a distance some 250 feet.

Phillips' continued the principle of multiple lifting surfaces with his 1904 'multiplane'. This untethered, piloted aircraft had 20 lifting surfaces, a cruciform tail unit, a tricycle undercarriage, and was powered by a 22 horsepower engine built by Phillips. This aircraft was demonstrated at Streatham and is claimed to have 'hopped' into the air, travelling a distance of around 50 feet, although it was particularly unstable

ABOVE
Horatio Phillips'
1904 Multiplane

about its longitudinal axis. Phillips' final attempt at flight came in 1907, using a larger version of his 1893 design. This aircraft had four sets of multiple-element wings, and was powered by a 22 horsepower engine turning a front-mounted propeller. This aircraft flew for a distance of some 500 feet on what is recognised as being the first powered flight in Britain. Longitudinal stability was, however, again considered to be very poor.

Chapter 4

Powered Flight

"I am convinced that human flight is possible and practical." – **Wilbur Wright, 1899**

"I confess that in 1901, I said to my brother Orville that man would not fly for fifty years... Ever since, I have distrusted myself and avoided all predictions." – **Wilbur Wright, 1908**

IT IS GENERALLY ACCEPTED THAT the term 'powered flight' refers to 'controlled, powered flight' made by 'heavier-than-air' flying machines. This distinction has to be made because 'lighter-than-air' vehicles had achieved powered flights some years before that of any heavier-than-air machine. In particular, the airship created by Count Ferdinand von Zeppelin had made its maiden flight over Lake Constance, near Friedrichshafen, Germany on July 2nd 1900. Acknowledged by most authorities, the Wright Brothers were the first to make a sustained, controlled flight of a manned, and powered, aircraft: others made heroic efforts in their attempts to become the first to fly.

The 'Nearly' Men

HIRAM STEVENS MAXIM, 1840-1916, was born in the United States but spent most of his adult life in England. In 1885 he demonstrated the world's first portable automatic machine-gun to the British Army. The 'Maxim Machine Gun' was widely used by the British, and other European, armies prior to World War I: the profits made Maxim a very wealthy man. He began to experiment with flying machines and, by the year 1893, had built a test vehicle to measure the amount of lift generated by different types of wings. With a wingspan of over 100 feet, and weighing around 7,000 pounds, the rig was powered by two 180 horsepower steam engines turning two propellers, each being over 17 feet in diameter. On July 31st 1894 the vehicle, together with Maxim and three other crew aboard, generated so much lift that it broke away from its restraining rails. The

machine was airborne for some 600 feet, and reached a height of around 3 feet, before crashing. Maxim's test rig did actually achieve powered flight, but the aircraft was certainly not controlled, and the flight was not sustainable.

Clément Ader, 1841-1926, was a French inventor whose most famous contributions to aeronautics were two remarkable aircraft known respectively as the 'Éole', and 'Avion No. 3'. The Éole was a bat-like monoplane, powered by a 20 horsepower steam engine turning a

BELOW Sir Hiram Stevens Maxim, with his machine gun invention

ABOVE
Augustus Moore
Herring experiments at
Lake Michigan in the
USA

single propeller. Ader claimed that on the 9th October 1890, while testing the craft on the estate of a friend near Paris, he flew the Eole a distance of 160 feet. Because the vehicle was overweight and under-powered, it only managed to bounce a few inches off the ground. Due to a fundamental design flaw, in that it lacked an adequate control system, the aircraft crashed, and was damaged beyond repair. Ader proceeded with the construction of Avion III,

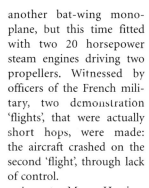

another bat-wing monoplane, but this time fitted with two 20 horsepower steam engines driving two propellers. Witnessed by officers of the French military, two demonstration 'flights', that were actually short hops, were made: the aircraft crashed on the second 'flight', through lack of control.

Augustus Moore Herring, 1867-1926, an American, built gliders that were inspired by the designs of Otto Lilienthal. These gliders typically included no control system other than by shifting the weight of the pilot, who was suspended beneath the wing. In 1898, Herring mounted a three-horsepower compressed air engine, driving two propellers, above the lower wing of one of his biplane gliders. Herring is reported to have flown his powered glider on two flights in October 1898. The first flight travelled 50 feet: a second flight, ten days later, lasted about ten seconds, and

travelled 72 feet. While Herring's craft probably did fly with an engine aboard, the craft was not manoeuvred by an in-built control system.

Gustav Weisskopf, 1874-1927, was born in Germany but moved to the United States where he changed his name to Gustave Whitehead. By 1898, he had built his first steam-powered aircraft. A single witness reported that Whitehead not only flew this aircraft in 1899, but had also covered a distance of 2,500 feet with the witness aboard as a passenger. There is no independent evidence to support this rather dubious claim, and it has been largely discounted. Around the turn of the century Whitehead built another aircraft, the No.21. This was a monoplane with a boat-shaped fuselage, weighing some 800 pounds, and powered with a four-cylinder gasoline engine turning two propellers.

On August 14th 1901, Whitehead was said to have made as many as four test flights of the No. 21, including one flight of up to seven miles in distance. Only one eyewitness could be found to corroborate the stories, some thirty years after the event, and this individual had a financial interest in a book being written about Whitehead. No photograph of his machine in flight has ever been found: Whitehead's rather feeble explanation being that, because his aircraft flew at speeds of up to 70 miles per hour, this was so fast that no camera could photograph him.

Richard Pearse, 1877-1953, was a New Zealander. An inventor, he spent most of his life developing various mechanical devices at his remote farm. Around the turn of the century, Pearse began to develop his aircraft, a monoplane, with a wingspan of 23 feet and powered by a 24 horsepower gasoline engine turning a single propeller. A simple system for aileron-like lateral movement, together with rudder and elevator controls, gave only limited manoeuvrability. There is much doubt about the year that the aircraft first flew. Some sources show it as being in 1901, while others claim it took place in either 1902 or 1903. Details of this first flight are even more confused, with unsupported claims of the aircraft travelling distances varying between 150 and 1,200 feet. Further flights were also said to have occurred in May and July of 1903, perhaps covering distances of up to 3,000 feet, and reaching altitudes over 30 feet.

However, there is little or no evidence to support these claims.

Preston Watson, 1880-1914, was a Scottish aviation enthusiast who was building and flying manned gliders in the early 1900s. His most interesting contribution to aeronautics was a new method of control called the 'parasol plane.' This device was a small second wing, placed above the main wing, that

could be rocked back and forth causing the aircraft to bank and turn. Watson incorporated this device into his later gliders, as well as in powered aircraft. Although local residents had recalled witnessing Watson making short, powered flights in a single-engine aircraft between 1903 and 1904, no one could remember any exact dates. Watson himself made no claim to have flown before the Wright Brothers, and documentation suggests he did not fly before 1905. He built two improved versions of his original powered aircraft, and both machines were flown frequently in the years before World War I. During that conflict, Watson volunteered for the newly formed Royal Naval Air Service, and was later killed when his aircraft exploded in flight.

The Wright Brothers

RIGHT Satellite image of Kill Devil Hills, taken in 2002. The dirt strip running from North to South toward the Wright Brothers' Memorial at the centre of the circular area denotes the distance travelled in their first flight

BELOW The Wright Brothers' 1903 Flyer during its first flight on December 17th, 1903 at Kitty Hawk, North Carolina. Orville Wright is at the controls and his brother Wilbur looking on

WILBUR WRIGHT, 1867-1912, AND his brother Orville, 1871-1948, were the third and sixth, respectively, of seven children born to Susan and Milton Wright. Milton was a minister in the United Brethren Church and the family moved frequently, until Milton became a bishop in the church, finally settling in Dayton, Ohio. On leaving school the brothers tried their hand at various occupations, including publishing newspapers and running a printing shop, all without great success.

In 1892, the brothers established a bicycle shop in Dayton that proved financially successful. They manufactured some bicycles under their own brand name, including a model they called The Flyer. During 1896, having read about the death of Otto Lilienthal, the Wright Brothers became intrigued with the subject of flight. They collected all possible information on flight, writing to Octave Chanute, the respected aeronautical theorist and scientist, who

was particularly generous with his advice. They also corresponded with Samuel Langley, Secretary at the Smithsonian Institute in Washington, DC. Langley had failed to fly his manned, but largely uncontrolled, flying machine the 'Great Aerodrome' only days before the Wright Brothers' success.

The Wrights designed a glider influenced by Chanute's designs, but devised their own method of flight control that included the technique known as 'wing warping'. In 1899 they tested a small-scale model of their glider in Dayton and, in the late summer of 1901, they were ready to test their first full-size glider. They chose an area of sand dunes known as Kill Devil Hills, outside a fishing village Kitty Hawk in North Carolina, as the test site. The glider flew successfully, but with much less lift than the brothers had calculated. A larger craft, with a control surface mounted in front of the wing, was also successfully flown, but their calculations showed inadequate lift was still a problem. This led them to design, and construct, their own wind tunnel facility at the rear of their cycle shop. A fan, driven by a gasoline engine, provided airflow through the tunnel. Within the tunnel, a series of

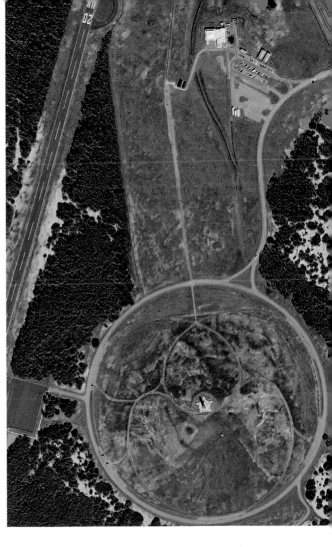

ABOVE The Wright Brothers, Wilbur and Orville

spring balances and scales measured the lift and pressure acting upon on their test aerofoils. In all, they tested over two hundred different aerofoil sections throughout November and December 1901. Their findings gave them an understanding of aerodynamic lift, in relation to the angle of attack of the aerofoil and its camber, together with the knowledge of how the controls required for flight could be achieved.

The Wrights used their newly acquired information in the design for Glider Number 3. This craft was equipped with a biplane wing and a canard elevator surface: a rear-mounted, fixed double-fin was later made adjustable, with its controls interconnected to the wing warping controls for the main wing. The pilot flew the aircraft lying in a prone position, on a small platform. On returning to Kitty Hawk in September 1902, they tested their new glider over more than one thousand flights. The outcome was successful, as they had predicted, and gave them the confidence to file a patent in March 1903, and begin the conversion of their glider into a powered machine. For this aircraft, the Wright Brothers built their own 12 horsepower gasoline engine that drove two aerofoil-section, contra-rotating propellers through gearwheels and bicycle chains.

On 14th December 1903, the brothers transported 'The Flyer' to the sand dunes of Kitty Hawk, North Carolina. The first flight attempt almost ended in disaster as, with Orville at the controls, the aircraft stalled and crashed to the ground, fortunately without serious damage to pilot or machine. After repairs, the brothers returned to Kitty Hawk to try again. The engine was started and, assisted by a falling-weight operated catapult, the aircraft moved forward along its guide-rail: 'The Flyer' historically, but briefly, lived up to its name as it became airborne, for a period of around 12 seconds, before settling to land on the dunes. Not an impressive beginning, but the Wright brothers had finally achieved one of mankind's oldest dreams. Throughout that same day December 17th 1903, the brothers made several more flights, improving with each flight as they gained confidence. Mankind had truly entered the age of powered flight.

Orville declared that the flight had been: "...the first in the history of the world in which a machine, carrying a man, raised itself by its own power into the air in full flight, had sailed forward without reduction of speed, and had finally landed under full pilot control". At first, the Wrights could only fly in a straight line for less than a minute. By the end of 1905, in a more powerful and modified version of The Flyer, they were flying figure-eight turns over Huffman Prairie, near their home at Dayton, often staying airborne for over half an hour, until their fuel ran out. Their 1905 version of The Flyer was the world's first practical, powered heavier-than-air flying machine.

BELOW A replica of the 1903 Wright Flyer takes off from a track on December 17th 2003, exactly one hundred years to the day, during the Centennial Celebrations of the First Flight at the Wright Brothers National Memorial in Kill Devil Hills, NC

Glenn Curtiss

GLENN HAMMOND CURTISS WAS born on May 21st 1878, in Hammondsport, New York. In 1900, Curtiss took over a bicycle and motor-cycle repair shop, a parallel with the Wright Brothers, and earned a reputation as a speedy cyclist and, later, motorcyclist as he became a champion in both fields. In 1903, he opened a factory producing very powerful engines and, in 1904, he established a land speed record of 67 miles per hour over a course of ten miles, a record that stood for seven years. In 1907, he set a new unofficial world record speed on a motorcycle of 136 miles per hour, an almost unbelievable speed at the time.

Curtiss met the Wright Brothers at the Dayton Fair in August 1906, and visited the Wrights' workshop where they discussed their common interests in aeronautics. The brothers did not show visitors their actual aircraft, as it was still not protected by patent. The Wrights were unaware that Curtiss had delivered an engine to Alexander Graham Bell, the famous inventor of the telephone, as part of a joint enterprise to build aeroplanes. Subsequently, there was much legal argument and litigation between the Wright Brothers and Curtiss. Their meeting at Dayton was cited as the source of Curtiss' knowledge of aeronautics relating to powered heavier-than-air machines and, thereby, infringed the patents filed by the Wrights. Curtiss counter-claimed that Samuel Langley's aircraft, the 'Great Aerodrome', had flown before that of the Wright Brothers, an event not proven in court.

His early experiments in aviation, together with Alexander Graham Bell, culminated in the flight of the 'June Bug' in 1908, for which Curtiss won the "Scientific American" trophy. This aircraft incorporated the best features of previous designs, including the ability to

take-off on a wheeled undercarriage using its own engine power, rather than the catapult launch method and the landing skids of the Wrights' aeroplane. The 'June Bug' had a strange-looking biplane wing arrangement, the lower wing having 'dihedral' (upward curved tips) while the upper wing had 'anhedral' (downward curved tips). Control was achieved by means of wingtip-mounted, triangular ailerons, instead of the wing-warping method used by the Wrights. Curtiss was later granted the first United States pilot's license in recognition of his achievement.

By 1910, the Wright Brothers had become very aware of the competition, often resorting to litigation against those with whom they competed. They formed an exhibition team to promote their products; several of their pilots were killed, as they became more adventurous in the quest for speed, altitude and manoeuvrability. Sales of the Wright Brothers' aeroplanes were less than expected, so the team was disbanded in 1911.

Wilbur Wright died of typhoid fever in 1912. By this time, the Wrights' aeroplane designs had stagnated to an extent that other makers, such as Curtiss in the United States, and most of the European companies, had overtaken them. Soon, European aeroplanes would be advanced beyond those of the Americans, as the shadow of imminent war descended.

LEFT Glenn Curtiss flying a modified version of Samuel Langley's 'Aerodrome' over Kenka Lake, New York in 1914

BELOW American aviation pioneer Glenn Curtiss and passenger sitting in one of Curtiss's highly successful floating planes in 1909

Chapter 5

Europe in the Air

"The most beautiful dream that has haunted the heart of man since Icarus is today reality." – **Louis Blériot**

Santos-Dumont

ALBERTO SANTOS-DUMONT, 1873-1932, was born in Brazil, one of three sons of wealthy parents. In 1891 he moved to Paris, France, where Alberto soon made his mark as an engineer, balloonist, dirigible airship pilot, and socialite. He knew Louis Cartier who designed a wristwatch for Dumont to wear while ballooning. In 1901, Alberto flew his Airship No. 6 around the Eiffel Tower, winning a prize of 100,000 francs that he promptly gave away to his mechanics.

In 1904, Santos-Dumont began to make heavier-than-air flights, initially in gliders. He also, unsuccessfully, built a helicopter in 1905, and in the following year built a flying machine, based on the plans for the Wright Brothers' biplane that had appeared in European magazines. In this machine, named the '14-bis' after the airship that carried it on its first public appearance, he made a flight that was the first, officially ratified, powered flight in Europe.

On November 12th 1906, observed by members of the Federation Aeronautique International (FAI), Santos-Dumont flew over a distance of 722 feet (220 metres), in a time of 21½ seconds, winning a prize of 1500 francs.

In 1909, after a series of failures, his fifth aircraft, the 'Demoiselle' became his first real success, even though it proved difficult to fly. This design was then given away, free, in the magazines, such as Popular Mechanics, in which the plans were published. This act of generosity provided a relatively inexpensive means to fly, for those aspiring to become aviators, and helped the growth of aviation in the early years. In 1916, he retired to Brazil where he died in 1932.

Samuel Cody

SAMUEL FRANKLIN CODY, 1867-1913, was born Samuel Franklin Cowdery in Iowa, United States, but moved to Britain in 1890. Originally a horse trainer, he later joined a Wild West Touring show where he demonstrated trick shooting and horse riding skills. Around this time he assumed the name Cody, in honour of his hero 'Buffalo Bill' Cody.

RIGHT
Samuel Cody's biplane 'Cathedral' in flight

BELOW
American-born British aviator Samuel Franklin Cody, at the controls of his aeroplane 'Cathedral' on Salisbury Plain

Cody began experimenting with man-lifting kites after British Army reports from the Boer War indicated that balloons, used as observation platforms, were useless in strong winds, and took a long time to inflate. He also crossed the English Channel, in a kite-powered boat, in 1903. The following year, Cody joined the Army on a temporary commission, at a salary of £1,000 per year plus expenses, to test his kites, as well as working on balloons and aeroplanes. In 1908, Cody built the British Army Aeroplane No. 1, and flew it himself on three occasions at Farnborough in that year

In 1909, Cody built a biplane that became known as 'The Flying Cathedral', referring to the curvatures of the biplane wings. By 1912, The Cathedral was capable of carrying up to four passengers at a time. Cody also had plans for an air ambulance version, for the Royal Army Medical Corps. Based at

MᴿCODY READY FOR FLIGHT.

F. SCOVELL. bd.

his workshop at Laffan's Plain, Cody spent many hours testing his aircraft in the skies over Farnborough, often observed by large crowds of onlookers. A memorial to Cody, a replica of the beech tree that Cody used for tethering his planes to, whilst testing engine thrust on Laffan's Plain, can be seen outside the Cody Building of the Defence Evaluation Research Agency (DERA), at Farnborough.

Louis Blériot

LOUIS BLÉRIOT WAS, BY ALL accounts, a dreadful pilot who was dogged by ill fortune in his attempts to become one of the great aviators of his time. Although a qualified engineer, Blériot had little knowledge of aviation. His personal fortune, gained from the manufacture of components for the automobile industry, was wasted on

failed attempts to design or fly aeroplanes. On one occasion, Blériot and Gabriel Voisin took one of their aeroplanes to a field in the Bois de Boulogne, Paris, where it promptly fell apart while taxying. That afternoon, on November 12th 1906, the same spectators who had witnessed Blériot's embarrassment saw Alberto Santos-Dumont fly his aeroplane, the '14-bis', on his historic flight, the first in Europe. Using borrowed money, Blériot entered the Daily Mail prize competition for the first aviator to cross the English Channel, in an aeroplane, in daylight. His aeroplane was smaller and less powerful than that of his competitors, with a wing-warping system for control, and had no instruments of any kind. The Anzani engine was crude, and splashed hot oil and smoke on the pilot, but was fairly reliable for its time.

ABOVE Louis Blériot's pilot's licence. Blériot was the first pilot to be granted an Aero-Club de France certificate

Early in the morning of July 25th 1909, and without the aid of a compass, Louis Blériot took off and headed out across the English Channel. Suspecting he had been blown to the North, he followed some ships heading, he had guessed, toward Dover. Blériot eventually crash-landed, as he often did, in a field near Dover some thirty-seven minutes after leaving Sangette, in Northern France. He had become the first to cross the English Channel and, as well as winning the prize money, he also became wealthy for a second time as a result of orders for his aeroplane. Following World War 1, and throughout the 1920s, Blériot's company manufactured a variety of products including, power boats, automobiles, motorcycles, carburettors, and furniture. Blériot had given up flying after sustaining serious injuries in a crash in 1910, and died of a heart attack in 1936.

Inspired by Blériot's success the city of Reims, in the Champagne region of France, sponsored a week of aviation competitions and exhibitions in August 1909, with large prize purses available to the winners of the major events. The major European manufacturers, at that time mostly French, entered various events. From America, Glenn Curtiss arrived with his 'Golden Flyer'. In the final of the top event, the Gordon Bennett Trophy, Curtiss took the hon-ours over two six-mile (10-km) timed circuits, beating the European flyers including Louis Blériot himself. Curtiss was hailed as "Champion Aviator of the World", in newspaper headlines from Paris to Dayton.

The Honourable C.S.Rolls

IN A PERIOD WHEN FLYING accidents were frequent, there were a number of fatalities among the early flyers. Charles Stewart Rolls, co-founder of the Rolls-Royce Company, was killed in the crash of a French-built Wright Flyer. Rolls had taken his first flight, in a balloon, in 1898. With Frank Hedges Butler and his daughter Vera, they formed the Aero Club (later Royal Aero Club), as an offshoot of the Automobile Club, with Rolls becoming a life-long committee member. He represented Britain in the 1906 Gordon Bennett Trophy for balloonists, taking-off from Paris, and landing 26 hours

LEFT French engineer and pioneer aviator Louis Blériot crosses the English Channel, the first by aeroplane, on 25th July 1909

and 18 minutes later near Sandringham, Norfolk. This feat came shortly after he had won the Tourist Trophy race for automobiles. C.S. Rolls' first powered flight came in November 1907, in the dirigible airship Ville de Paris.

Rolls had been in communication with the Wright Brothers since March 1906. When the brothers flew at Le Mans, France, in 1908, Rolls was an interested spectator and, on October 8th, he flew in an aeroplane for the first time. Having first taught himself to fly gliders, he then made a solo powered flight before the end of 1909. In March 1910, he was given the second Pilots Certificate awarded by the Aero Club. His greatest aeronautical achievement came on June 2nd 1910, when he made the first non-stop, two-way crossing of the English Channel. Only a few weeks later on July 12th, he was killed, following structural failure of his Wright Flier at the Bournemouth Aviation Meeting. Perhaps best remembered for his part in co-founding the company Rolls-Royce, which itself has played a significant role in the history of aviation, Rolls had

THE LITTLE BOOK OF FLIGHT | 49

accomplished so much in his comparatively short lifetime. As acknowledged in Flight magazine: "Although only 33 years of age, Mr Rolls had already done what it has fallen to the lot of very few men to do, and what only a very small percentage of men are capable of doing, whatever may be their opportunities."

J.T.C Moore-Brabazon

JOHN THEODORE CUTHBERT Moore-Brabazon was born in England, on February 8th 1884. He made his first solo flight in a French Voisin biplane at Issy-les-Montineaux, Paris, in November 1908. In the following year, Brabazon made the first livestock cargo flight by aeroplane when, having first tied a basket to a wing-strut of his Voisin biplane as a 'cargo hold', he airlifted a small pig.

BELOW Lord Brabazon, holder of the first British flying licence

In October 1909, Brabazon won the first all-British competition for a prize of £1,000, offered by the Daily Mail, for the first machine to fly a circular, one-mile course. In the same year, Michelin offered £1,000 for a long-distance flight: Brabazon, who covered a distance of 17 miles, also won this prize. The FAI issued him with brevet No.40, under the incorrect name of 'Brabazon Moore', on March 8th 1910. The Aero Club (later the Royal Aero Club) awarded him British Pilot's Certificate Number 1,

Claude Grahame-White

CLAUDE GRAHAME-WHITE WAS born at Bursledon, in Hampshire, England, on August 21st 1879. He had been a yachtsman, motoring enthusiast, and automobile dealer, before his interest in aviation was sparked at the Reims meeting of 1909. He ordered a Blériot Model XII two-seater monoplane and, in order to become familiar with the construction of the machine, had enrolled as a worker in the factory at Neuilly-sur-Seine. On the morning of delivery, and without the instructions on how to fly the machine which were yet to be delivered, he started the machine and flew for a few short hops. He then had the aeroplane taken to Pau where, with the help of a flying instructor named Leblanc, on January 4th 1910, he received the first French licence, 'No. 30', to be awarded to a Briton. In April of that same year, he was awarded British licence 'No. 6', on the strength of the licence gained in Pau.

making him the first person to be licensed in Great Britain as an aeroplane pilot. In World War I, Brabazon took a leading role in the development of aerial photography. In World War II, he chaired a Cabinet committee that was to explore, and advise upon, what Britain's post war airliner needs would be. One of the designs arising from this became the Bristol Type 167, which was named the 'Brabazon' in his honour. Lord Brabazon of Tara died in London, on May 17th 1964.

ABOVE Aviation pioneer Claude Grahame-White takes off from Executive Avenue, outside the White House, Washington DC, in a Farman III biplane on 4th October 1910

After the demise of the Model XII, the only one of its type, in a crash while being piloted by Louis Blériot himself, Grahame-White returned to London and established a flying centre at Hendon. He later attended the Henry Farman flying school at Chalons, in France, where he learned to fly the Farman biplane. In this aircraft he attempted to win the £10,000 prize, offered by the Daily Mail, for the first aviator to complete the journey from London to Manchester, a distance of 183 miles, within 24 hours. His first attempt failed after landing in a field at Lichfield, Staffordshire, where his aeroplane was blown over in high winds. After returning to London to repair his aeroplane he, and a competing aviator, the Frenchman Louis Paulhan set off from London on April 27th 1910, within a few hours of each other. Paulhan landed near Lichfield where he refuelled, and also spent the night. Meanwhile, Grahame-White was beset with engine problems and, despite

British raid by naval aircraft on Zeebrugge. He later resigned his commission and returned to the management of his business interests, manufacturing his own design aircraft and building others under licence, all of which were crucial to the war effort. His Hendon aerodrome was taken over by the Air Ministry, and is now the main site of the Royal Air Force Museum. Grahame-White emigrated to California, where he dealt in real estate, eventually returning to Europe where he died, in Nice, France, on August 19th 1959.

attempting to catch Paulhan by flying at night, was forced to abandon his attempt when he landed not far from where his first attempt had failed. Louis Paulhan flew on to Manchester where he duly claimed the Daily Mail prize.

Grahame White was the first English pilot to carry mail in Britain, and the first to fly at night. In 1910 he won the Gordon Bennett Trophy Race in the United States. During World War I, he was commissioned in the Royal Naval Air Service, and took part in the first

BELOW Louis Paulhan in his Henri Farman III, at Lichfield during the Daily Mail 1910 London to Manchester air race

Chapter 6

Magnificent Men & Their Fighting Machines

"Aviators live by hours, not by days."
– T. H. White

AT THE BEGINNING OF WORLD War I, in August of 1914, the aeroplane was only a little over ten years old. The Blériot XI, in which Louis Blériot first crossed the English Channel, was only five years old, yet it had already gone to war, in 1911, with Italian forces in North Africa.

The Airborne Scout

AT THE OUTBREAK OF THE GREAT War, the Royal Flying Corps (RFC) took twenty-three Blériot XI aircraft into

pilots carried pistols and rifles into the air, and began to shoot at each other. In some cases, machine guns were fitted on a ring-mount, and fired by a second crewmember.

LEFT Royal Aircraft Factory SE5 scout aircraft of 1917

Guns in the Air

ON APRIL 1ST 1915 A FRENCH pilot, Roland Garros, shot down a German Albatros aeroplane. Although this was not the first air-to-air kill, Garros' monoplane, a Morane Parasol, was the first aeroplane that was modified for the purpose of aerial combat. Working with Raymond Saulnier, its designer, Garros had developed reinforced propeller blades that deflected bullets from a forward-firing machine gun. Using this system, Garros proceeded to shoot down five German aeroplanes in a fortnight. His success led to the introduction of an interrupter mechanism that allowed the gun to fire through the arc of the propeller, without the need for such reinforcement, a system that Saulnier had been developing prior to Garros' bullet deflectors.

Garros' aircraft fell into enemy hands after he was shot down, and unable to

France, where they served as reconnaissance aircraft with six RFC squadrons. The French Service de l'Aviation also utilised Blériots in eight of their 'escadrilles', while Italy went into action with six squadrons of Blériot XI aeroplanes. At first, aeroplanes were not considered as fighting machines but used as airborne 'scouts', allowing observations of enemy troop movements and positions from the comparative safety of altitude. These scout aircraft were initially unarmed, and pilots from opposing forces were reported as having waved at each other as they flew by. This situation did not last for long: soon the

destroy his aeroplane before being captured. Within two days Anthony Fokker, the Dutch engineer, had devised a workable interrupter mechanism. For a period, the German aces Immelman and Boelke, and their fellow airmen, controlled the skies as they flew their Fokker Eindekker monoplanes that were armed with synchronised Spandau machine guns. The Allies soon introduced their own synchronised guns, thus redressing the balance of air power.

In 1916, the British introduced the Sopwith 1½ Strutter, and the French, the Nieuport 17. Both combined the synchronised gun system with more powerful engines, and began to dominate the skies. The Sopwith Camel, armed with two synchronised Vickers machine guns, arrived later that year, and proved to be an excellent fighter, shooting down over 1200 German aircraft. Unfortunately, many airmen were killed while learning to fly it. This did little to improve morale of British pilots whose life expectancy was just over two weeks.

The Triplanes

PROGRESS IN AIRCRAFT DESIGN and technical innovation went hand-in-hand, as the allies and their opponents developed newer, faster, and better-armed aircraft. These developments included aeroplanes such as the Sopwith Triplane, and the Fokker Dr1 (Drei-dekker) triplane. These aircraft were noted for their exceptional manoeuvrability, this feature being an essential part of any air combat if the pilot was to survive for very long.

Fighter tactics changed throughout the war, as the pilots fought out their aerial battles. Pilots attained almost legendary status for their exploits: the Allies had aces such as Major Edward 'Mick' Mannock, Colonel William Avery 'Billy'

Bishop, Capt. James McCudden and Capt. Albert Ball, together with René P. Fonck from France, Edward 'Eddie' V. Rickenbacker from the United States, and others. Their German opponents included the fabled Manfred von Richthofen, otherwise known as 'The Red Baron', Oswald Boelcke, and Max Immelman.

The Zeppelin Raiders

STRATEGIC AERIAL BOMBING originated during World War I when German Zeppelins began raiding London, from their bases in occupied Belgium. At the start of the war, the German Army had seven military Zeppelins: each could attain a maximum speed of 136 kilometres per hour, and a height of 4,250 metres. Armed with five machine-guns, they could also carry 2,000 kg (4,400 lbs) of bombs.

In January 1915, two Zeppelins flew over the East Coast of England, and bombed Great Yarmouth and King's Lynn. The first Zeppelin raid on London took place on May 31st 1915, killing 28 people and injuring 60 more. Many places suffered from Zeppelin raids included Gravesend, Sunderland, Edinburgh, the Midlands, and the Home Counties. By the end of May 1916, at least 550 British civilians had been killed as a result of Zeppelin raids. Although the Zeppelins could carry out successful long-range bombing attacks, they were extremely vulnerable to both gunnery attack, and bad weather. British fighter pilots and ground-based

ABOVE LEFT
Captain Albert Ball, a Royal Flying Corps hero of World War I. Credited with 44 victories, mostly on lone missions, he was shot down and killed aged only 20 years

ABOVE
German First World War air ace Manfred von Richthofen, known as the Red Baron, with a comrade in front of his famous Fokker tri-plane

anti-aircraft gunners became very successful at bringing down Zeppelins. The use of incendiary bullets in machine-guns had a devastating effect as the hydrogen gas, used to fill the lift envelopes of the airships, was ignited when the Zeppelin came under fire. Of the total of 115 Zeppelins used by the German military, 77 were either destroyed or damaged beyond repair. By June 1917, the Zeppelins were withdrawn from bombing raids over Britain.

Zeppelins of the German Naval Airship Service made a total of 159 sorties over Britain, killing 557 people, and inflicting a massive amount of damage to property. Count Ferdinand von Zeppelin died of pneumonia on March 8th 1917, at the age of seventy-eight. Peter Strasser, the Chief of the Naval Airship Division and the driving force behind the German airship program, was aboard the Zeppelin L70 when it was shot down over the English Channel on August 5th 1918: this event, effectively, signified the end of the airship as a strategic bomber.

The Aeroplane as a Bomber

IT IS NOT KNOWN EXACTLY where, or when, explosive devices were first dropped from aeroplanes. However, there is evidence to suggest that the bomber came into use before the advent of the fighter. Before hostilities began in 1914, the French, Germans, Russians, and Austro-Hungarians were developing aircraft specifically designed to carry bombs, and release them onto a target. The British had also experimented with the dropping of bombs from aircraft before the war, but the construction of aircraft designed specifically for the purpose did not commence until after the outbreak of hostilities.

Virtually all types of aeroplanes, including observation aircraft and fighters, were used on bombing missions at some time during the war. The British De Havilland DH-4, for example, could carry either an observer, or bombs, but not both. This aircraft was later modified with a more powerful engine, better armament, and could carry more bombs, thus becoming one of the most successful aircraft later in the war. There was an urgent military requirement to develop much larger, longer-range aircraft that would be able to penetrate enemy defences, defend themselves from aerial attack, and then deliver a greater load of bombs onto targets that were often far behind the battlefront.

The first purpose-built bomber to be used in an aerial bombing mission was the French 'Voisin V', a pusher biplane, which attacked and bombed the Zeppelin hangers at Metz-Frascaty on August 14th 1914. The Voisin was a strong, well-built aircraft with a steel airframe, and was initially powered by a 70 horsepower engine, with a bomb load of around 132 pounds. Later versions were fitted with a 155 horsepower engine, with the bomb load rising to around 660 pounds.

The Imperial Russian Air Service was equipped with the 'Ilya Mourometz', designed by Igor I. Sikorsky. Originally a civil transport, the Ilya Mourometz was an improved version of the 'Russky Vitaz', the world's first four-engined aeroplane that first flew on May 13th 1913. Protected by a defensive armament of three or four machine guns, it

was very difficult to attack and often shot down its opponents. Coupled with innovations in bombing, namely a bomb-aiming device together with an internal bomb bay, this aircraft was a great improvement over the earlier, visually aimed and hand-held bombing method. A success rate of around 60 percent of bombs on target proved effective, especially when compared to the poor results obtained by the 'drop it over the side of the cockpit' method.

The British also began building an effective purpose-built bomber. In

ABOVE French built Voisin 'pusher', originally built for reconnaissance, but later developed as a bomber. The Voisin is credited with the first air-to-air kill

OPPOSITE LEFT German Zeppelin caught in searchlights during a bombing raid

December 1914, the Admiralty Air Department ordered the development of an aeroplane with which to bomb Germany. The specification was for a two-seat, twin-engine aircraft, capable of a speed of at least 75 miles per hour, and a load of a minimum of six 112-pound bombs. This resulted in the Handley Page O/100, which entered service with the Royal Naval Air Service in November 1916, and was used at first for daylight sea patrols. With a crew of four, this aircraft could carry sixteen 112-pound bombs, and could have its wings folded to fit into standard hangars. With machine-guns fitted in the nose, dorsally, and firing downward from the lower fuselage, it served effectively until the end of the war, carrying out night bombing of German U-boat bases, railway stations, and industrial sites.

The Germans meanwhile, in the autumn of 1916, had developed what later emerged as their most infamous bomber of World War I. In order to carry out a long-range bombing campaign against Britain, and as the effectiveness of the Zeppelin diminished, they needed a new aircraft for that purpose. It came in the form of the Gotha G-V, structurally different from its predecessor, the Gotha IV, and was fitted with more powerful Mercedes engines. The G-V could carry more than 1,000 pounds of bombs, and had a downward 'firing tunnel' through the bottom of the fuselage that enabled the rear gunner to protect the bomber from fighter attack from below.

The Italians produced the three-engine Caproni Ca.3 biplane bomber in 1914, the prototype powered by Gnome rotary engines. The production version was equipped with three 100 horse-power in-line Fiat A10 engines, and entered service in the summer of 1915. It was said to have been one of the most effective bombers of any air force. The later Caproni triplane bombers, the Ca.4 series, were armed with up to eight machine-guns, and were capable of carrying large bomb loads to distant targets, mainly at night. The Royal Naval Air Service used six of the Ca.4 bombers during 1918.

The Aircraft Carrier

THE FIRST AIRCRAFT CARRIER, HMS Ark Royal, had been launched in 1914. Converted during build as a merchant vessel, she served in the Dardanelles, and elsewhere. The first strike from an aircraft carrier against a land target took place on July 19th 1918. Seven Sopwith Camels, launched from HMS Furious, attacked the German Zeppelin base at Tondern, destroying several airships and balloons.

As the war progressed, the aeroplane had evolved from the flimsy, hand-built, and barely controllable, machines of the Wright Brothers and their contemporaries. It had become much more reliable, manoeuvrable, and controllable, was capable of flying at greater speeds and higher altitudes, and could cover great distances without stopping for fuel. These advances in aircraft design and construction, although the legacy of war, would soon be used by man to explore new horizons, and open up new avenues to the rest of the world. All that was needed were men and women with the vision and desire to continue the progress of flight.

BELOW Sopwith 2F1 Camels on the deck of HMS Furious. Seven of these aircraft were flown off the carrier in July 1918 to bomb two Zeppelins in their sheds at Tondern

Chapter 7

History Makers & Record Breakers

"Ours is the commencement of a flying age, and I am happy to have popped into existence at a period so interesting."
– Amelia Earhart

MOST OF THE POST-WORLD WAR I aviation record attempts were sponsored by rich businessmen who offered large cash prizes, and impressive trophies, as incentives to the world of aviation. Men and women took up the gauntlet of challenge: some succeeded, others failed, often with fatal consequences.

The Schneider Trophy

JACQUES SCHNEIDER, THE SON OF a French arms manufacturer, became one of the officials in the French gov-

ernment responsible for the development of aviation. Schneider decided that, as much of the earth was covered with water, and many major cities were located on ocean shores or along rivers, aeroplanes should have the ability to land on water, either on pontoons (seaplanes), or on hulled fuselages (flying boats). As an incentive, Schneider proposed an international competition for the 'Coupe d'Aviation Maritime Jacques Schneider', later known as the Schneider

Cup, although it was actually a silver trophy. Schneider also hoped that a French aviator would win the trophy.

The rules of the competition reflected Schneider's intentions, in that competing aeroplanes had to first float on the water for six hours, and then prove their seaworthiness by travelling a distance of about 550 yards on water. During the flight phase, aeroplanes had to twice "come in contact with" the water. If a team won three races within five years,

they would retain the cup, and the winning pilot would receive 75,000 francs. Each race was to be hosted by the previous winning country, and supervised by the Fédération Aéronautique Internationale, together with the Aero Club of the hosting country.

The first contests had been held in 1913 and 1914, both off the coast of Monaco. The aeroplanes competing in those years were land planes, modified with pontoons fitted to the underside of the fuselage. Maurice Prevost, a French pilot, won the first race in a Deperdussin, having achieved a speed of 126 miles per hour, and was the only pilot to finish. The following year, a Sopwith Tabloid land-plane, equipped with pontoons and piloted by Howard Pixton, won the race for the British. The event was resumed after the war in 1919, off the English coast at Bournemouth: the Italian team won, but was later disqualified, and the race declared void.

The race was run annually, between 1920 and 1927, and thereafter two-yearly: this was to allow more time for development, as aeroplanes were becoming more complex. The annually held races were won by Italy (three times), Britain, and the United States (twice each). In the 1927 race, the British government financed the winning Supermarine S5 entry that was flown by RAF pilots. In 1929 at Cowes, the British won again in a Supermarine S6 powered by a new Rolls-Royce engine. Incredibly, the British government withdrew its support for the 1931 event. Fortunately, a private donation of £100,000 by Lady Lucy Houston, who had inherited her shipping magnate husband's £6m fortune in the 1920s, enabled a British Supermarine S6B to win the Schneider Trophy outright, at the same time setting a new world airspeed record of 407.5 miles per hour.

The Atlantic Challenge

THE ONSET OF WORLD WAR I HAD put a stop to many potential aviation record attempts. In 1913, Lord Northcliffe, publisher of the Daily Mail, had offered a prize of $50,000 dollars for the first aviator to cross the Atlantic. Northcliffe had recognised how difficult this feat would be as, in the original rules, the aircraft was allowed to land on the water, could be refuelled, and even towed for repairs, as long as the flight

BELOW
US Navy Curtiss NC-4

BELOW A Curtiss NC-4 receives an inspection

was resumed from the point of touch down. The only aircraft with any real chance of success would have to be a seaplane or flying boat and, at that time,

Glenn Curtiss manufactured the best seaplanes and flying boats.

Curtiss built two flying boats, and prepared to fly one, named 'America', to Newfoundland for the attempt which, after many delays, was set for August 15th 1914. The outbreak of war on August 4th put a stop to the record attempt, but the British Admiralty was so impressed with the performance of the planes that it ordered sixty of them for maritime patrol. In 1919 the Daily

LEFT Vickers Vimy cockpit configuration showing the proximity of propellers to the pilots (8 inches), photographed from the wing struts of a replica aircraft in 2001

Mail renewed the challenge, but now the flight had to be non-stop, and without refuelling or landing.

The United States Navy decided to attempt the Trans-Atlantic flight anyway, "...for scientific purposes". Originally accompanied by two other flying boats, the Curtiss NC-4 commanded by Albert Cushing Read left Newfoundland on May 16th 1919, and reached the Azores 15 hours later. The other two aircraft both put down at sea due to rough weather and their crews rescued by ships. After repairs, the NC-4 took off again and landed in Lisbon, Portugal on May 27th, becoming the first aeroplane to cross the Atlantic under its own power, in 26 hours total flying time.

Alcock and Brown

BACK IN NEWFOUNDLAND, TWO teams worked feverishly in preparation for what they considered the ultimate challenge: the Daily Mail prize of $50,000 dollars, for the first non-stop crossing of the Atlantic, had still to be claimed. One team, led by Admiral Mark Kerr, prepared their Handley Page V/1500 'Berlin Bomber' fitted with four powerful Rolls-Royce engines, the largest aircraft built by the Allies during the war. However, due to problems with engine cooling, their attempt was delayed.

The second team was preparing a Vickers Vimy, originally a night bomber that was produced too late for the war. The pilot was Captain John Alcock, and the navigator was Lieutenant Arthur

VICKERS-VIMY-ROLLS.

THE FIRST DIRECT FLIGHT ACROSS THE ATLANTIC.
JUNE.14-15.1919.
CAPT: SIR JOHN ALCOCK K.B.E. D.S.C.-PILOT.
LIEUT: SIR ARTHUR WHITTEN BROWN K.B.E-NAVIGATOR.

Whitten-Brown. Both had spent the later years of the war in a German prison camp; therefore, neither had accumulated much flying experience, especially with so large an aircraft. Whitten-Brown was originally an air observer, and had taught himself aerial navigation while a prisoner. On the morning of June 14th 1919, Alcock and Brown took off.

During the flight, Brown had to climb out onto the wings, six times, to chip off ice that formed there. On several occasions, Alcock had to descend low over the sea, hoping that the warmer air, at lower altitude, would melt the ice that kept forming in the engine intakes. On two occasions, Brown made what he thought would be his final entry into the flight log and put it inside his shirt, hoping it would thus be available if his body were ever to be found. Sixteen and a half-hours later, on the morning of June 15th, the Vimy landed in a bog near Clifden, in Ireland. People on the ground tried to wave them away from the bog, and direct them to a prepared landing field, but Alcock and Brown just waved back. The Vimy landed in the bog and pitched its nose into the soft mud. Alcock and Brown duly collected the prize money, and were also knighted. Alcock was killed later in the same year, on December 18th 1919, while flying the new Vickers Viking amphibian to the Paris air-show, when its wing struck a tree. Brown never flew again, and died on October 4th 1948.

R.34

IN 1919 A THIRD CROSSING OF THE Atlantic took place, this time by a British dirigible airship R.34 that was a copy of a captured German Zeppelin, the L.33. The crossing was a two-way flight, the R.34 becoming the first aircraft to cross the Atlantic both ways. This heralded the beginning of regular airship services across the Atlantic.

LEFT A poster commemorating Alcock and Brown's direct flight across the Atlantic. The poster reads 'Vickers-Vimy-Rolls: The First Direct flight Across The Atlantic June 1919 Capt Sir John Alcock KBE DSC Pilot Lieut Sir Arthur Whitten Brown KBE Navigator'

ABOVE Charles
Lindbergh (third from
right) and his Ryan
aircraft the Spirit Of St
Louis shortly before his
record breaking solo
Trans-Atlantic flight

OPPOSITE RIGHT
Amelia Earhart

Charles Lindbergh

ALSO IN 1919, A FRENCHMAN
named Raymond Orteig, owner of two
Manhattan hotels, put up a prize for a
Trans-Atlantic flight. Orteig hoped the
prize would be an incentive to French
fliers, and would also lead to France
again becoming a leading nation in
world aviation. Originally, the rules set a
five-year time limit that was later
extended. However, there was no stipu-
lation of solo flight.

Charles Augustus Lindbergh was
born on February 2nd 1902, in Detroit.
His early aviation career had included
both barnstorming, and air mail delivery. When the Orteig prize was
announced, Lindbergh tried unsuccessfully to interest aeroplane manufacturers Bellanca and Fokker to supply him
with an aircraft for the attempt. With
the financial help of some St. Louis
businessmen, who insisted that the
aeroplane be named after their city,
Lindbergh contracted the Ryan Aircraft
company of San Diego to modify one of
their standard single-engine aircraft to
his specifications. The Ryan, named the

'Spirit of St. Louis', was stripped of all unnecessary equipment, with only a periscope for forward visibility and was, effectively, a flying fuel tank. It was also very unstable in flight.

Lindbergh took off from Roosevelt Field, New York, in the early morning hours of May 20th 1927, when there was an unexpected clearing in the weather. After thirty-three and a half-hours of pinching himself, and often opening the side window to let in cold air to keep him awake, Lindbergh landed in Paris. Although he was the ninety-second person to cross that ocean, he gained international fame as the first person to fly 'solo' across the Atlantic, at the same time setting a distance record of 3,614 miles. Charles Lindbergh died in Hawaii on August 26th 1974.

Amelia Earhart

AMELIA EARHART WAS NICK named 'Lady Lindy' because her achievements were comparable to those of Charles Lindbergh. Considered by many as "the most celebrated of all women aviators", she was born on July 24th 1897, in Atchison, Kansas. After

paying a pilot one-dollar, for a 10-minute aeroplane ride, she made the decision to become a pilot and join this predominantly male field. After her first ride, she wrote, "By the time I had gotten two or three hundred feet off the ground, I knew I had to fly." Taught to fly by Neta Snook, the first woman to graduate from the Curtiss School of Aviation, Earhart received her pilot's licence from the FAI in October 1922. Soon after, on October 22nd 1922, Earhart set a women's altitude record of 14,000 feet in a Kinner Canary, an open-cockpit, single-engine biplane.

Earhart became the first female to cross the Atlantic Ocean. Leaving Newfoundland, Canada, on June 4th 1928, Earhart joined Wilmer L. Stutz and Louis E. Gordon in their bright red Fokker

ABOVE Amelia Earhart stands in front of her bi-plane called 'Friendship' in Newfoundland, 1928

F.VII, named the 'Friendship', on their 2,000-mile trip to Wales. Earhart had no part in piloting the plane during the twenty hours and forty minutes trip and was, in her own words, "just baggage." This made her even more eager to cross the Atlantic solo. Four years later, she became the first woman pilot to cross the Atlantic, setting a new time record of 14 hours and 56 minutes. Later, in 1935, she flew solo from Hawaii to California, a distance greater than that from the United States to Europe.

In an attempt to be the first to do so, in 1937 she decided to fly around the world. With her navigator Fred

Noonan, she took off in her twin-engine Lockheed Electra from Miami, Florida, and headed east, assisted by high altitude winds. With two thirds of the journey completed, the Lockheed vanished somewhere between New Guinea and Howland Island, in the Pacific. Their disappearance remains one of the great mysteries of aviation. Amelia Mary Earhart died doing what she most loved, just a few days before her fortieth birthday.

The Australian Adventurers

THE 1919 ENGLAND-TO-AUSTRALIA race offered a prize of £10,000 to the first aviator and crew who could fly the 8,400 miles in 30 days, or less. Two logical routes to Australia existed, one across Europe and much of Asia, and one through North America and across the Pacific. Australian officials believed that the Europe and Asia route was much safer, because it was over land for most of the way, and would still provide a very challenging exercise in navigation.

Several Australian aviators entered including Bert Hinkler, Charles Kingsford-Smith, and two brothers, Ross and Keith Smith. Hinkler wanted to fly the trip solo, but race officials believed that the journey would be too dangerous for a lone aviator, and forced him to withdraw. Charles Kingsford-Smith, planned to take a crew of three with him. However, neither he nor his crew could navigate very well, and race officials also barred them from the competition. With only a few contestants, the Smith Brothers became the favourites to succeed. On November 12th, Ross and Keith Smith took off from Hounslow, London, in a Vickers Vimy. Landing in Darwin on December 10th 1919, the brothers and their two mechanics completed the flight from Hounslow in 27 days and 20 hours. The brothers each received a knighthood for the achievement, and a cheque for £10,000, which they insisted on sharing equally with their mechanics.

Bert Hinkler was still smarting from being barred from the race, and remained determined to fly to Australia alone. He subsequently bought an Avro Avian biplane to replace the Sopwith that his sponsors had withdrawn, when

he was barred from the 1919 race. On February 7th 1928, Hinkler left England following broadly the same path that the Smiths had flown in 1919. He made good time, landing in Darwin on February 22nd after fifteen and a half days, a little more than half the time of the Smiths' flight. An instant national hero, Hinkler received a special £2,000 prize from the Australian government.

Like Hinkler, Charles Kingsford-Smith was also upset about being excluded from the 1919 contest, and wanted to blaze his own flight path to Australia. His dream was to fly the Trans-Pacific route. Smith met a fellow Australian aviator named Charles Ulm, who shared his desire to fly across the Pacific. Searching for an Australian sponsor for their endeavour, Smith and Ulm decided to prove their skills by flying the entire Australian coastline, a journey of some 7,500 miles, in just over ten days, earning £3,500 in spon-

sorship from the New South Wales government. The previous record was 22 days, 11 hours. On reaching the United States, Smith and Ulm selected a Fokker trimotor plane for their flight. However, because of political upheaval back home, the two men had to return their sponsorship money to the Australian government. Fortunately, they met an American steamship line owner who was intrigued by the idea of their Trans-Pacific flight. He purchased the Fokker, and gave it to them. They named it 'Southern Cross', after the constellation in the Southern Hemisphere that would help them navigate at night. To complete their crew, Smith and Ulm selected Harry Lyon, a ship's captain, as the navigator, and James Warner as the radio operator.

On May 31st 1928, Southern Cross took off from Oakland, California. The trip consisted of three legs, via Honolulu, Suva Island in Fiji, and finally to Australia. Although encountering some dangerous squalls on the final leg, the aircraft landed in Brisbane on June 10th 1928, to the cheers of more than 15,000 spectators. The actual in-air flight time for the journey was a little more than 83 hours.

Smith went on to set more aviation records. In October 1930, he flew solo from London to Australia in 9 days 22 hours, beating Hinkler's record by more than five and a half days. Then in 1934 he, and fellow Australian P.G. Taylor, flew the same Trans-Pacific route that Smith had flown in 1928, but in the reverse direction, from Australia to San Francisco, becoming the first to fly from Australia to the United States, via the Pacific. On November 10th 1935, Kingsford-Smith and his co-pilot died while trying to set another England-to-Australia flight record, when they crashed into the sea in the Bay of Bengal during a monsoon.

Kingsford-Smith, Hinkler, Ross and Keith Smith, and their crews had proved that Australian pilots were among the best in the world, and also opened up Australia to international air travel and commerce.

Chapter 8

Aviation for the Common Man

"I suppose we shall soon travel by air-vessels; make air instead of sea-voyages; and at length find our way to the Moon, in spite of the want of atmosphere." – **Lord Byron, 1822**

IN THE LAST YEAR OF WORLD WAR I a practical, non-military, use of the aeroplane occurred when the United States Post Office carried mail, initially between Washington, Philadelphia, and New York, in May 1918, extending to Chicago and California by September 1920. Similar operations began in Europe in 1919, with passenger flights between European capitals. The governments of England, Italy, and Germany and, to a lesser extent, Russia began to convert to civil use some of the large bombers that were completed too late for the war, and thereby recoup some of their costs.

LEFT The Italian Caproni Capronissimo on Lake Maggiore, Italy, 1921. With quarters for 100 passengers, it was the largest aircraft in the world, but destroyed by fire before it flew

The Barnstormers

IN AMERICA, IN THE PERIOD after World War I, aeroplanes could be purchased cheaply due to the release by the military of surplus training aircraft such as the Curtiss JN-4 'Jenny', and the Thomas-Morse 'Scout'. As a result, aviators were to be found almost everywhere in the American countryside. These fliers often slept out in the field under the wings of their machines, fixed their own aircraft, and flew passengers on 'joyrides' in turn for money for a meal, or to buy fuel. There were also flying circuses and 'barnstormers', who were so named after their stunt of flying through the middle of open-ended barns. One of the most successful of these barnstorming acts, pilot Ormer Locklear and his promoter William Pickens, introduced to the paying public such feats as wing walking, the act of jumping from car to aeroplane, and vice versa. Locklear even exchanged aircraft, simultaneously with another pilot, by jumping between the wings as the aircraft flew close together.

ABOVE
Ormer Locklear, wearing a tuxedo, walks on the wings of an aircraft, crashed in a farmer's field in a still from director James P. Hogan's silent film, 'The Skywayman'. Locklear died while performing an aerial manoeuvre during shooting for the movie

Imperial Airways

THE WORLD OF FLIGHT WAS SOON to become available to the general public. In Britain, in 1923, a Government Committee recommended that subsidies given to aircraft companies that operated air services should be withdrawn, and the companies merged into one organisation. With the purpose of developing commercial air transport on an economic basis, and to create a company that would be strong enough to develop Britain's international air services, Imperial Airways Limited was formed on March 31st 1924. On the next day, it took over the aircraft and services of Handley Page Transport Limited, The Instone Air Line Limited, The Daimler Airways, and British Marine Air Navigation Company Limited. Imperial Airways inherited 1,760 miles of cross-Channel routes, and a collection of aircraft, most of which were obsolete. Their land aircraft operations were based at Croydon Airport that had opened on March 25th 1920.

Imperial Airways had the twin tasks of re-opening European air routes, and also establishing air links between Britain and the Empire. These varied routes required aircraft to be designed to operate them: the Empire routes would additionally require major planning, to overcome difficult flying conditions and extremes of climate. Industrial disputes with the pilots delayed the start of services until April 26th 1924, when a daily London-Paris service was opened with a De Havilland

sengers, and 212,380 letters. The start of the Empire routes in 1926 saw a large increase in the company's fleet. A Handley Page W9, a three-engine, fourteen passenger aircraft, and four Handley Page W10 twin-engine, sixteen passenger aircraft were delivered in March. In July, the new Armstrong Whitworth Argosy introduced a new standard of comfort, and roominess, into air passenger transport when it came into service. On May 1st 1927, an

DH34. Routes between Southampton and Guernsey, and London to Brussels, Ostende, and Cologne followed a month later and, in the summer, a service from London to Basle and Zürich, via Paris.

One of the first aircraft to enter service with Imperial Airways was the Handley Page W8F 'City of Washington', a single engine, eight passenger aircraft having a range of 365 miles. In its first year of operations the company aircraft flew 853,042 miles, carried 11,395 pas-

AVIATION FOR THE COMMON MAN

Argosy inaugurated the world's first 'named' air service, the London-Paris 'Silver Wing' service, on which meals were served. Argosies also operated on routes to Basle, Brussels and Cologne. The first of the new de Havilland Hercules airliners, ordered specially for the Empire routes, began a service between Egypt and India on December 20th. The following year, 1928, a new route between Cairo and Basra began. As an aid to navigation across the featureless desert, a furrow of several hundred miles in length was ploughed in the sand.

The year 1929 saw the start of the first flying boats in service between Britain and India, with the entry of the Short Calcutta, a three-engine, fifteen passenger aircraft with a range of 650 miles. Services to the African continent soon followed. Not all routes were operated entirely by flying boats, land based aircraft often being used for parts of the journey. On April 1st 1931, the first experimental London-Australia airmail flight took place, the mail arriving in Sydney some 26 days later. In 1931, two four-engine airliners came onto the scene: the first of three Short S17 Kent flying boats, 'Scipio', operated routes in the Mediterranean, whilst the first of the Handley Page H.P.42 aircraft, 'Hannibal', operated initially between London and Paris, and later on the Egypt, India and Africa routes. These airliners brought a new standard of

feature was its promenade deck. On October 30th 1936, the first of the Empire-class flying boats 'Canopus' made its inaugural service flight on a Trans-Mediterranean service. The aircraft was a success, and further orders for a total of 42 were placed.

LEFT Imperial Airways 'Canopus' at Short's factory in Rochester, Kent

European Air Transport

AIR TRANSPORT IN EUROPE WAS also developing at a great rate. In 1926 the Germans had created Deutsche LuftHansa, renamed Lufthansa in 1934. Equipped with the latest aircraft produced in the Junkers factories, LuftHansa established a strong market throughout Europe. The company soon established a subsidiary in South America, VARIG, which overtook the French company Aéropostale as the major carrier between Europe and South America. The French national airline Air France was established in 1933 and had an extensive route network, not only across Europe, but also to French colonies in North Africa, and elsewhere.

service, comfort, and safety to passengers, with stewards serving high quality meals amid Pullman style luxury.

The Short S23 Empire flying boat has been described as being '…without question the most famous and successful of all pre-war civil transports'. The S23 usually carried 24 passengers or, 16 in a sleeping berth layout. A popular

Composite Aircraft

THE VAST DISTANCE ACROSS THE North Atlantic had seemed an almost insurmountable barrier, preventing the start of air services westwards to Canada and the USA. One method used to increase aircraft range resulted in experiments with the Short-Mayo 'Composite' aircraft, the brainchild of Major Robert Mayo of Imperial Airways, which first flew in 1937. The concept was simple: a powerful but light 'mother' aircraft, a modified Empire Class flying boat 'Maia', would take off carrying a small four-engine seaplane 'Mercury' on its back: at altitude, the smaller aircraft would be released, and fly on to its destination. By this means the range and payload of the smaller aircraft could be maximised. This long-range concept was proven with non-stop flights from Britain to both Canada, and South Africa; Mercury still holds the world distance record for floatplanes. Sadly, both aircraft were lost during World War II.

BELOW Short-Mayo Composite 1938: A seaplane, the 'Mercury', sits on top of an Imperial Airways flying boat, the 'Maia'

The Airship

THE FIRST AIRSHIP CROSSING OF the Atlantic was made in 1919 by the British R-34. However, dirigible airships gained notoriety in a series of spectacular disasters. In 1920, the R-38 airship broke up and crashed in flames into the River Humber. The R38 was on its fourth, and final, trial flight that was to have been combined with its official United States Navy acceptance flight. A total of 44 men, British and Americans, lost their lives. Another airship, the R-34, was damaged beyond repair while on a test flight in 1921. The Roma, built in 1922 by Italy for the United States, crashed and exploded over Hampton Roads, Virginia, and a French-operated Zeppelin obtained from Germany, the Dixmude, was lost in the Mediterranean in 1923. In 1925, the United States Navy airship Shenandoah was destroyed by violent winds: its two successor airships were also destroyed, the Akron in 1933, and the Macon, in 1935.

There were some remarkable flights by airships, notably that, in 1929, when the German airship Graf Zeppelin flew around the world in less than 21 days. Problems such as structural failures, coupled with the effects of winds and weather, continued to beset the airship.

ABOVE The R100 airship on the mooring mast at Cardington, Bedford in 1929

The hydrogen gas, that gave it lift, often fuelled a beacon fire that marked the end of an airship. In 1930, while on route to Egypt, the British Airship R-101 exploded after crash-landing in France, with the loss of 48 passengers and crew. Perhaps the most spectacular disaster involved the German airship Hindenburg. After making ten Atlantic crossings on scheduled commercial flights in 1936, it was destroyed by fire in 1937, while landing in Lakehurst, New Jersey, killing 35 people on board and one ground crew member. This event effectively ended the era of the airship in commercial aviation.

Airlines in America

ON JULY 15TH 1916, WILLIAM Boeing had formed his aircraft manufacturing business as Pacific Aero Products Company, changing the name to the Boeing Airplane Company a year later. In 1927, Boeing Air Transport was formed to operate mail and passenger services between Chicago and San Francisco. By 1928, with 800 employees, Boeing had become one of the largest aircraft manufacturers in the United States.

AVIATION FOR THE COMMON MAN

The late 1920s and the 1930s saw a rapid growth in air transport, with the formation of many small operators that won contracts for airmail deliveries across the United States and overseas. Many were amalgamated into larger companies that became known the world over. Pan American Airways began airmail services in 1927. Flying boats were used to link the United States with South America, and later on routes across the Pacific and Atlantic oceans using both the Martin M-30 Clipper, and the larger capacity Boeing 314 Clipper aircraft. The Sikorsky S-42 flying boat was introduced by Pan American Airways in 1934, on the Buenos Aires route, carrying 32 passengers on a typical flight.

American Airways, later to become American Airlines, began operations in 1934, using Curtiss T-32 Condors on the New York to Miami route. Within a few years, however, the Condors were replaced by DC-2s and DC-3s, and were no longer used on the main routes. Continental Airlines can trace its roots to Varney Speed Lines, which was formed in 1932; the name was changed to Continental Airlines in 1937. United Airlines began in 1931, as the holding company of four mid-1920s US carriers: Boeing Air Transport, Varney Air Service, Pacific Air Transport, and National Air Transport. The Boeing Model 247 airliner was introduced into service with United Airlines in 1933.

The passenger-carrying airlines thus began to have an impact on the travelling public worldwide. Many people would soon see the advantages of air travel over existing surface transport, particularly over long distances, and increased frequency of services.

BELOW United Airlines timetable front cover from June 1931

Chapter 9

Preparing for War

"Air power may either end war or end civilisation."

– Winston Churchill, 1933

THE VERSAILLES TREATY OF 1918, ending World War I, demanded the destruction of the German military. Specifically, it ordered the destruction of all warplanes, and prohibited any kind of air force. When Adolf Hitler and his National Socialist (Nazi) party came to power in 1933, they stealthily began the process of rearming, while openly campaigning against the Versailles Treaty restrictions. On March 10th 1935, Hermann Goering summoned the military attaches of Britain and France to his grandiose offices in the Air Ministry building in Berlin. He informed them that Germany no longer considered itself bound by the restrictions placed on its development of military aircraft under the Treaty of Versailles. This was followed by a flypast of German aircraft

The Spanish Civil War

IN THE YEARS BETWEEN THE world wars there was only one major military conflict, the Spanish Civil War. On July 17th 1936 General Francisco Franco, and soldiers loyal to him, seized a Spanish Army outpost in Morocco. In Spain, other Nationalist troops quickly seized other garrisons. A junta of generals, led by Franco, declared themselves the legal government, and the war began.

Many countries, including the Britain and the United States, stayed neutral, in their belief that participation would lead to escalation of the war. Some groups and individuals from neutral countries volunteered for service with the Republican forces, including a small group of Americans who became the Patrolla Americana. The Soviets offered equipment, soldiers, and senior advisors, and sent aircraft such as the Polikarpov I-15 and I-16 to serve with the Republican Air Force. France also provided some aircraft and artillery. The Republicans utilised civilian aircraft such as the Lockheed Orion, which

that had been produced in violation of the treaty. However, some of these aircraft were old, civilian aircraft that had been painted in military colour schemes, one of the ploys adopted by the Germans to convince their adversaries that they possessed a greater force than was actually the case.

The British, French and Americans resorted to their drawing boards, and readied their factories, to try to catch up with the perceived lead of the Germans. The British, in particular, were shocked by the demonstration of apparent German air power: the notion that they would have at least ten years advance warning of imminent war had led to the research and development of aircraft and weapons, in Britain, falling into decline.

Wolfram von Richthofen, a cousin of 'The Red Baron,' was equipped with the most modern aircraft and specially trained staff. Many of the newest aircraft were sent to Spain, among them the Heinkel He111 bomber, and the Messerschmitt Bf109 fighter. The Condor Legion successfully evacuated a large number of Franco's troops from Morocco, where they were blockaded by the Republican navy, to Seville in Spain. This involved a fleet of twenty Junkers Ju52 trans-

ABOVE
Junkers Ju-52 Tri-motor on display at the Smithsonian Air and Space Museum in Dulles, Virginia

were adapted to military use, and also used a Boeing P-26 that had been brought from the United States before the war for demonstration to the Spanish Air Force.

Italy was quick to support Franco's Nationalist forces, and sent to Spain more than 700 aircraft during the conflict. Franco had also sent a request for help to Adolph Hitler. The Germans, as well as providing 'volunteer' ground troops, seized the opportunity to test its Luftwaffe aircraft and crews in a real combat situation. The Condor Legion whose chief of staff was Colonel

ports and took two months, with the loss of only one aircraft. It was the first major airlift of troops in military history. Hitler later declared that "…Franco ought to erect a monument to the glory of the Junkers 52. It is this aircraft that the Spanish revolution has to thank for its victory"

The Condor Legion used both tactical and strategic bombing during the conflict, notably at Guernica, in Northern Spain, where saturation bombing devastated the city, and left many inhabitants dead. Ironically, the only military target in town, a bridge, remained untouched. The greatest effect of the bombing was to make some European nations become fearful that they would be the next Guernica, and thus capitulate to Hitler's demands at Munich in September 1938. Soon, veterans of the Spanish Civil War would be flying over Poland, Czechoslovakia, France, and other European countries, as part of an experienced, well-trained air force, fighting for Hitler.

Britain Prepares

BY THE MID-1930S THE POLITICAL situation in Europe could no longer be ignored. Britain eventually reacted to the situation, and recognised the need to rapidly increase the capability of the Royal Air Force. This was achieved in several ways, initially with the introduction of new aircraft that were based on reworked existing designs and, subsequently, by totally new aircraft that were built to fulfil particular roles. The new initiatives led to the introduction of many new types of aircraft, both in Britain and elsewhere, around the middle of the decade. In particular, the

LEFT
The Boulton Paul Overstrand, a medium bomber which was the first RAF bomber to be fitted with the new power-operated turret

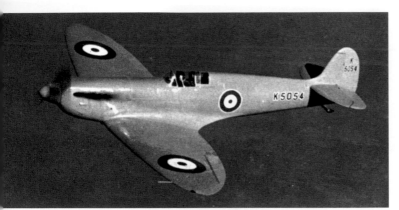

September 1935. This aircraft met the requirement for a fighter aircraft, even though it was obsolete before it left the factory. Later, small numbers were ordered as attrition replacements, and a batch of three hundred Gladiator Mark II aircraft were ordered as a 'stop-gap', due to development problems with the Rolls-Royce Merlin engine that was to power the forthcoming Spitfire and Hurricane. Although outdated, the Gladiator later served with distinction in several theatres of war, particularly in the defence of Malta in 1940, and in the Norway campaign with the Fleet Air Arm.

year 1935 saw the debut of many aircraft that went on to secure their place in history in the dark days of the coming war.

In the early 1930s H.P. Folland, Chief Designer of the Gloster Aircraft Company, carried out a re-appraisal of his earlier design, the Gauntlet, in order improve its performance. The result was the Gloster SS37, later named 'Gladiator', a single-engine biplane fighter. In a joint venture with Hawker Aircraft, the Gloster machine was approved for the immediate production of an initial batch of twenty-three aircraft, and a second batch of one hundred and eighty was ordered in

The Hawker Hurricane was the brainchild of Hawker's chief designer, Sydney Camm, who decided, in 1933, to design a monoplane fighter based on the Fury biplane. The Hurricane had a retractable undercarriage, fabric covered fuselage and wings, and was intended to have a Rolls-Royce Goshawk engine. The Hurricane was later fitted with metal-skinned wings, a three-bladed propeller turned by a

Rolls-Royce Merlin engine, and armour plate to protect the pilot. With its eight machine guns and rugged construction, it was an effective weapon, particularly in the early years of the war.

The design of the Supermarine Spitfire drew heavily on the experience gained with the Supermarine S6B, winner of the Schneider Trophy. An immediate predecessor, the Type 224 that was designed by R.J. Mitchell to meet an Air Ministry specification, failed to gain a contract. Mitchell was given a free hand to design a new single-seat fighter, without the encumbrance of an official specification. Its sleek fuselage was designed around the Rolls-Royce Merlin engine; the wings had a distinctive elliptical plan form and contained eight machine guns, as well as housing the retractable main undercarriage. The result was to become one of the most famous aircraft of all time.

The United States

IN APRIL 1934, THE U.S. ARMY AIR Corps invited bids for a multi-engine bomber that could carry a bomb load of 2,000 pounds for at least 1,020 miles, at a speed of 200 miles per hour. Boeing proposed the four-engine Model 299, with its all-metal construction and a bomb bay that could carry 4,800 pounds of bombs. It was heavily armed with a gun turret in the nose, two side gun positions, and a ball-turret on the bottom of the fuselage. When rolled out on July 28th 1935, it was nicknamed the 'Flying Fortress' because of its heavy armament.

The Bell Aircraft company was formed in 1935. The following year, it started design work on a radical new high-altitude fighter, the P-39 Airacobra. It had a single-engine mounted behind the pilot with the front-mounted propeller driven by a long shaft, a tricycle undercarriage, and self-sealing fuel tanks. A 37-millimetre calibre cannon was mounted within the propeller hub, and two 7.62-millimetre machine guns were fitted in the fuselage. The aircraft, with different armament, was later ordered by the British Purchasing Commission but proved unsuitable for its role as a fighter, due to a poor rate of climb. It served successfully with Russian forces, both in air combat and ground attack duties, and with United States forces in the Pacific and North Africa.

Originating from the DC-2 and DST (Douglas Sleeper Transport) aircraft that were derived from the DC-1 prototype that first flew in 1933, the DC-3 had entered airline service in the United States in 1936. The military saw its potential after acquiring some production DC-2s in 1936, and modifying them for use as an Army personnel and cargo transport. The Army advised Douglas Aircraft of the changes needed to make it suitable for its wider requirements, namely, more powerful engines, strengthened rear fuselage with large

BELOW
Bell P-39 Airacobra of the RAF. Note the 37-mm cannon in the propeller hub

ABOVE
Douglas DC-3 airliner
of United Air Lines

cargo doors, and a reinforced cabin floor. This aircraft, although a product of the 1930s went on to perform duties with military and civilian operators for many years: some are still flying in the 21st century.

The Luftwaffe

THE JUNKERS JU87 STURZKAMP-fflugzeug dive-bomber, otherwise known as the 'Stuka', first flew in early 1935. The Stuka later became renowned for its successes in the German campaigns in Poland, Crete, North Africa, and on the Eastern Front, during World War II. One of the major developments that helped the Stuka pilots achieve deadly accuracy, without them being killed in the process, resulted from its operations in the Spanish Civil War. While flying in Spain it was found that pilots would actually 'black out', and lose control of their aircraft, while attempting to pull up from a steep dive. On one occasion a whole formation of Ju87s was late in pulling up, and several hit the ground. The Ju87B, therefore, was fitted with an automatic mechanism that pulled the aircraft out of a steep dive, at a predetermined altitude: it also had a more powerful engine. Sirens were installed on the fixed landing gear and created a terrifying screaming noise, as the aircraft dived toward its target, the noise having almost as much effect as the bombs it carried.

Willy Messerschmitt designed a low-wing monoplane with retractable landing gear, leading-edge slats, and enclosed cockpit. These features,

together with its all-metal, flush-riveted, monocoque fuselage made the Messerschmitt Bf109 the most modern of the contenders for the German fighter contract. Originally intended to be powered with the Junkers Jumo engine, it was fitted with a Rolls-Royce Kestrel when rolled out in September 1935. This aircraft was eventually to serve the Luftwaffe until the end of the war, becoming one of the greatest fighters of its day.

With no previous design experience of twin-engine military aircraft, Messerschmitt commenced work on the Bf110 just a year later. Designed to a 1934 requirement for a long-range escort fighter to be powered by two Daimler-Benz DB600 engines, which were not yet available, the first prototype Bf110 made its initial flight on May 12th 1936 with two Junkers Jumo engines, each developing around 610 horsepower. When it entered service, as the Bf110C in 1939, it was fitted with two 1100-horsepower DB601A engines.

The original Junkers Ju52 started life as a single-engine cargo transport aircraft. Only six of the single-engine Ju52s had been built before the company had decided to evaluate a three-engine configuration. The Junkers design team, under

Ernst Zindel, undertook work to adapt the airframe of the seventh Ju52. This was converted to take three 550-horsepower Pratt & Whitney Hornet 9-cylinder radial engines, becoming designated Ju52/3mce. When first flown in April 1931 it was such a success that the single-engine version was discontinued, in favour of the Ju52/3m Dreimotoren (three motors). The Ju52 was used by civil airlines around the world, but the Luftwaffe developed it as a military transport, paratroops carrier, and also as a bomber with three bomb bays.

One of the most successful, and versatile, German aircraft of its time was the Junkers Ju88. The prototype Ju88 flew on December 21st 1936, following a 1935 specification for a three-seat, high-speed bomber. This aircraft was subsequently used throughout the war as a bomber, reconnaissance aircraft, and night-fighter.

Other civil aircraft with military potential were either modified, or used as the design basis for later purpose-built warplanes. The Dornier Do17, originally intended for Lufthansa as a six- passenger mail aircraft, formed the basis for the Do217 medium bomber that first flew in 1938. Similarly, the Heinkel He111 started out as a civilian airliner with Lufthansa, but it was designed with military use in mind, the third civil prototype being modified to become the prototype of the bomber variant that was used in great numbers in the coming conflict.

BELOW
Leaving their base for a raid, German Heinkel HE 111 bombers

Chapter 10

War in the Air

"Believe me, Germany is unable to wage war."
– Former British Prime Minister David Lloyd George, 1934

AROUND DAWN ON SEPTEMBER 1ST 1939, Germany launched its attack on Poland. On September 3rd 1939, Britain and France declared war on Germany.

Airborne Offensive

THE LUFTWAFFE CARRIED OUT several major airborne assaults during World War II, that of Holland in 1940, and Crete in the following year, being the most notable. In both cases the troops were transported in the Junkers Ju52 aircraft, and in gliders. The ability to deliver both troops and supplies, by air, proved a valuable asset to both sides throughout the war.

Battle of Britain

AFTER THE FALL OF PARIS IN 1940, and the evacuation of British troops from Dunkirk, Germany was in control all across mainland Europe. Britain

weeks, the skies above England became an aerial battlefield. Waves of German bombers, and their escorting fighters, mounted many attacks in their attempts to overcome the resistance of the Royal Air Force. Hurricanes and Spitfires were

braced itself in preparation for the inevitable attacks that would precede invasion: the German air attacks began in early summer. Hitler had recognised that, in order to invade Britain, the Luftwaffe must first control the skies. Starting on July 10th 1940, the Luftwaffe attacked shipping convoys in the English Channel, and bombed Channel ports: they also attacked the radar stations at Dover, Rye, and Pevensey, but failed to destroy them. One of the aircraft types used in these raids was the Junkers Ju87 'Stuka' dive-bomber that was particularly successful early in the war, when there was no effective fighter opposition. However, when dive-bombing, they were vulnerable to attacks by Hurricanes and Spitfires, and were withdrawn from the battle by mid-August.

A renewed offensive began on August 13th 1940 and, in the following three

toward the Russian front, and elsewhere. The heroic efforts of the RAF pilots were recognised in the speech by Winston Churchill, when he said: "Never before in human history was so much owed by so many to so few."

pitched in battle against the German Me109s escorting the Heinkel and Dornier bombers, whose bombs threatened the airfields and installations below. The skies over the south east of England were filled with the vapour trails left by the combatants and the smoke from bursts of anti-aircraft fire from the ground.

Later in the German offensive the attacks were directed against London, both by day and at night, in an unsuccessful attempt to demoralise the population into surrender. Large numbers of bombers were used in the 'Blitz', protected by waves of fighters. By September, Hitler had cancelled plans for invasion, and turned his attention

Pearl Harbour and the Pacific

IN DECEMBER 1941, THE JAPANESE attack on Pearl Harbour shocked not only America: the world was suddenly aware of the military might of Japan,

and the effectiveness of her carrier-based aircraft. At the time of the attack, the Nakajima B5N2 'Kate' torpedo bomber was the best in service with any of the world's navies. One hundred and forty-four aircraft of this type participated in the Pearl Harbour onslaught, as they laid waste to the Pacific Fleet and the airfields of the defenders. During the following year, carrier-based 'Kates' sank three American aircraft carriers, while others supported Japanese amphibious landings in the Pacific. As war progressed, the Japanese lost their dominance in the air, partly due to heavy losses of pilots, and also the lack of newer aircraft to combat those introduced by the Americans.

In mid-1943, the United States Marine Corps introduced a new fighter, the Chance Vought F4U Corsair. In August, carrier units began to use the new Grumman F6F Hellcat, a fighter that had been built to counter the Japanese Mitsubishi A6M Zero fighter, arguably the finest shipboard fighter in the world during the early years of war in the Pacific. The Zero took part in every major action that involved the Japanese Navy, from Pearl Harbour to the final assault on Japan. Later, the

LEFT
Grumman F6F Hellcats of the American Airforce in WW II

Lockheed P-38 Lightning, while less manoeuvrable than the F4U or the F6F, used its superior speed and altitude capabilities to good effect, as it shot Japanese aircraft out of the air.

Russia and the Eastern Front

OPERATION BARBAROSSA BEGAN at dawn on June 22nd 1941, when 30 bombers attacked airfields in western Russia. Stalin had ignored the warnings from both the British and his own intelligence service of the imminent attack, and refused to relocate his air force units: 1,489 aircraft were destroyed on the ground on that first day. By the end of the first week, more than 4,000 aircraft of the Soviet air force, the VVS, had been destroyed. The Russians introduced new aircraft types as they resisted attack, and later fought valiantly, notably in the defence of Stalingrad. Two of the new models were the MiG 3, a high-altitude interceptor fighter, and the Ilyushin IL-2 Sturmovik, a low-altitude attack aircraft with easy handling and powerful armament. The Sturmovik was a devastating ground attack aircraft, particularly effective against the German Panzer units.

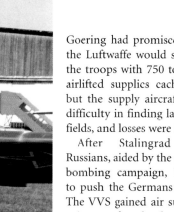

Goering had promised that the Luftwaffe would supply the troops with 750 tons of airlifted supplies each day, but the supply aircraft had difficulty in finding landing fields, and losses were high.

After Stalingrad the Russians, aided by the Allied bombing campaign, began to push the Germans back. The VVS gained air superiority as, for the last two years of the war, it grew larger, and began to operate many types of aircraft from the Lend-Lease program including Hurricanes, Spitfires, B-25 Mitchells, and Bell Airacobras. One pilot, A.I. Pokryshkin, became Russia's second-highest scoring ace while flying an Airacobra P-39. The Soviet factories were now producing large numbers of newer and deadlier aircraft, such as the Petlyakov Pe-2 light bomber, and the Yakovlev Yak-9 anti-tank and escort fighter. The already excellent Sturmovik was further improved, and had a tail gunner position added, thus surprising German pilots as they attacked from the rear. Gradually, the Germans were pushed back to Berlin. They had attacked a country unprepared for war, and weakened by its politics, but allowed it to fight back and claim victory. The Soviet nation and its air force had experienced a rebirth, and emerged from World War II as a global power prepared for the imminent Cold War.

America at War

DURING THE EARLY DAYS OF World War II, before the United States officially became a combatant nation, some Americans had independently joined the Royal Air Force. Forming the Eagle Squadrons, they fought alongside British pilots in the Battle of Britain, and other early conflicts. In the Far East, through the Lend-Lease program, China received Curtiss P-40 Tomahawks. Mercenary instructors and pilots known as 'The Flying Tigers' flew these powerful, low-altitude fighters. Some of these pilots had lied about their flying achievements, claiming fighter experience when they had flown only bombers or trainers: the salary of $500 a month was nearly double that of the average military pilot, with a bonus of $400 per confirmed kill.

The Boeing B-17 Flying Fortress proved essential to success in Europe, delivering half of all bombs dropped in that theatre. They operated in Britain, as part of the 8th Air Force, and in North Africa, and the Pacific. The first Boeing B-29 Superfortress mission of the war was flown from India on June 5th 1944, against Japanese-held Bangkok. When the Marianas Islands were recaptured, the 20th Air Force relocated there, bringing Japan within flying range of the B-29. A conventional bombing campaign against Japan, that included both conventional high explosive and incendiary bombs, was followed by the dropping of the first atomic bomb on August 6th 1945, by the B-29 'Enola Gay', on the city of Hiroshima. Three days later a second nuclear bomb was dropped, by the B-29 'Bock's Car', on Nagasaki. The Japanese surrendered a week later.

The best American fighter of the war, and possibly the best propeller-driven fighter ever flown, was the North American P-51 Mustang. The RAF, in 1940, was eager to procure more aircraft, and offered a contract to North

American to build Curtiss P-40 Tomahawks with Allison engines. Because the licensing fee to Curtiss-Wright was too high, North American offered to build a fighter for the RAF that would surpass the P-40. The offer was accepted, on the condition that a prototype of the aircraft would be ready 120 days later.

On October 4th, only 102 days after accepting the challenge, the prototype was ready except for its Allison V-1710 engine. The first test flights were eventually held on October 26th, but the prototype was damaged when the pilot took off with an empty fuel tank, and the engine cut out shortly after take-off. The Mustang generally performed better than the P-40, but it did not climb well, and performed poorly at higher altitudes. In September 1942, British engineers saw that the engine housing of the Mustang could accommodate the new Rolls-Royce Merlin engine. With the Merlin powering it, the Mustang became a legend.

Women Fliers in Wartime

THROUGHOUT WORLD WAR II, women contributed to the war effort in many ways, earning the gratitude and respect of society, and furthering the cause of the women's movement. The Soviet Union, which already had a tradition of women in combat, was the first nation to use women as pilots. After suf-

ABOVE Boeing B-29 Superfortress bomber Enola Gay at the Smithsonian Museum. The Enola Gay dropped the atomic bomb on Hiroshima, Japan

OPPOSITE LEFT North American P-51D Mustang fighters flying in formation over Italy in World War II

fering huge battle casualties in 1941, the government ordered all women without children, who were not already engaged in war work, to join the military. There were three all-woman regiments: fighter, bomber, and night bomber. Other women flew with male regiments, and one such pilot, Valentina Grizodubova, became the commander of a 300-man, long-range bomber squadron. Soviet women were the only female combat pilots of the war: one of them, Lilya Vladimirovna Litvyak, known as 'The White Rose of Stalingrad', became an ace, downing 12 German aircraft before she was shot down in 1943. Twenty-three women were given the Hero of the Soviet Union medal.

No German women flew in combat, but some took their part in wartime aviation. Melitta Schiller was awarded the Iron Cross for completing 1,500 test dives of new dive-bombers, and Hitler favourite, Hanna Reitsch, a record-breaking glider and test pilot before the war, test flew virtually every Luftwaffe aircraft. Britain used women pilots of the Air Transport Auxiliary (ATA) to ferry aircraft between factories and operational units. In the United States, record-breaking pilot Jacqueline

Cochran tried to use her influence to form a woman's squadron, but seeing that it was becoming hopeless, she took a group of women pilots to England to fly with the British ATA.

Jet and Rocket Aircraft

THE FIRST TEST of a jet-propelled aircraft took place in Germany at Rechlin on July 3rd 1939, when test pilot Erich Warsitz flew the Heinkel He176 in the presence of Hitler, Goering, Udet, and the entire Luftwaffe High Command. The test was successful but the Nazi hierarchy thought the device was either a hoax, or a joke. The Luftwaffe refused to sponsor its development: therefore, the Heinkel Company did so, privately.

The first prototype of the rocket-powered Me163 Komet was completed

during early 1941. Flight testing began in the spring of 1941, with a series of unpowered flights before the aircraft was taken to Peenemünde West, for installation of a 1,653 pounds thrust Walter RII-203 rocket motor, and its first powered flights. It finally entered service in 1944, but was not a great success.

The first British jet aircraft flew on May 15th 1941, when Jerry Sayer piloted the Gloster-Whittle E.28/39 on its successful first test flight. Frank Whittle, the engine designer, was knighted as a result. Before the war ended, both the Germans and the Allies put jet aircraft in the air. The Germans had both the Messerschmitt Me262 Schwalbe (Swallow), and the Heinkel He162 Volksjaeger (People's Fighter). The British flew the Gloster Meteor, and the Americans, the Bell P-59A Airacomet. These were all impressive achievements in aeronautical engineering, but had limited usefulness in the war, as they all arrived too late to have any real part in the outcome.

Chapter 11

Jump Jets and Jumbos

"If you are in trouble anywhere in the world, an airplane can fly over and drop flowers, but a helicopter can land and save your life."

– Igor Sikorsky, 1947

IT BECAME ESSENTIAL TO THE commerce and economy of most major cities to have an international airport nearby. This prompted the building of new, larger airports that were needed to handle the increasing numbers of passengers drawn to air transport, and also to serve the larger aircraft that were being built to satisfy the demand.

Commercial Airliners

IN THE YEARS IMMEDIATELY AFTER the end of World War II, commercial airlines used modified ex-military aircraft, and older pre-war airliners.

Among these were Douglas DC-3s, which flew in the war as the C-47 Skytrain transport, the Avro Lancastrian, a modified Lancaster bomber, and the Douglas DC-4 Skymaster that had first flown in 1939 and had served in large numbers as the C-54 during the war. New aircraft including the Boeing 377 Stratocruiser that was based on the B-29, but with a new fuselage, and the Lockheed Super Constellation, entered service before 1950. Followed by the DC-6 and DC-7 developments of the DC-4, the Americans established a strong foothold in civil aircraft manufacturing.

In Britain, aircraft designers concentrated on the ill-fated Saunders-Roe Princess flying boat and the Brabazon airliner, both obsolete before their first flights. However, they also produced some significant new designs that changed the world of commercial passenger aircraft. These were the Vickers Viscount medium-range airliner that first flew in July 1948 powered by four Rolls-Royce Dart turbo-propeller engines, and the De Havilland Comet four-engine airliner, the world's first jet airliner to enter service in early 1952. A major setback to the Comet, resulting from a series of catastrophic crashes, needed a redesign of the window apertures, from rectangular to round in shape, and other modifications.

LEFT
Vickers Viscount turbo-propeller airliner undergoing high altitude trials over Mount Kilimanjaro in East Africa in June 1950

BELOW
De Havilland Comet prototype airliner on 19th December 1949. The rectangular window apertures were changed to round in later versions following structural failures that led to catastrophic crashes

ABOVE Air New Zealand Boeing 747

The resultant delays, together with adverse publicity, led the airlines to look elsewhere: in 1954 Boeing introduced its new four-engine passenger jet aircraft, the Boeing 707, with the support of a large order from Pan Am. The 707 began commercial service in 1959; further orders rolled in, giving Boeing the lead in the market. Douglas produced its DC- 8, and the Convair Company their 880/990 series, but Boeing's dominance of the civil airliner market continued. Their 727, and later the 737, became the most numerous civil airliners in service, worldwide. With the advent of the Boeing 747 'Jumbo jet' in 1969, the company was the world's lead-

ing airliner builder, although Lockheed with its Tristar, and McDonnell Douglas's DC-10 and MD-11, achieved limited success in the marketplace. Toward the latter part of the twentieth century, the European Airbus consortium began to challenge Boeing with a range of Airbus aircraft and, in 2003, overtook it to lead the market.

Berlin Airlift

THE USE OF TRANSPORT AIRCRAFT in situations such as humanitarian relief was brought to prominence during the Berlin Airlift when, in June 1948, the

routes. The airlift officially ended on September 30th 1949. During the entire operation 17 American, and seven British planes were lost due to crashes.

The Berlin Airlift carried greater significance than simply victory against the Soviets, as it became the model for future humanitarian airlifts. Aircraft specifically designed for air cargo transport were later introduced: the Lockheed C-130 Hercules, C-141 Starlifter, C-5 Galaxy, and more recently the Boeing C-17 Globemaster III, were all produced in response to the experience gained, with benefit to both civil and military airlift operations.

The Korean War

AFTER THE NORTH KOREANS HAD invaded South Korea in 1950, and following the United Nations decision that a policing force be sent, the situation soon developed into all-out war. Smaller-scale tactical bombing followed strategic air attacks by American B-29 bombers, based in Guam, on industrial targets in North Korea. As the war progressed, jet fighters replaced the piston-engine Mustangs, Corsairs, and Sea Furies. Soon

Soviet occupation forces in East Germany blockaded all ground supply routes leaving only three 'air corridors', that were protected by treaty, into West Berlin. In a massive operation, initially by American and British military transport aircraft, and later with those from Australia, South Africa, and New Zealand, the Allies kept the Berlin population supplied with basic foodstuffs, coal, medical supplies, machinery, soap, and newsprint. They also delivered 23 tons of treats for the children in West Berlin. On May 12th 1949, after more than 2.3 million tons of cargo had been carried on 277,685 flights, the Soviets relented, and reopened the ground

the jet-powered Lockheed F-80 Shooting Stars and North American F-86 Sabres, of the United Nations forces, fought dogfights with their opponents, the Soviet-built Mikoyan-Gurevich MiG-15, in the notorious 'MiG Alley' area of Korea. On November 8th 1950, 1st Lt. Russell Brown, flying an F-80, shot down a MiG-15 in the first all-jet dogfight in history.

Airlift techniques used in the Berlin Airlift were perfected during the Korean conflict. Supplies of food, ammunition, medical equipment, jeeps and guns were parachute-dropped from Fairchild C-119 cargo aircraft: the Douglas C-124

Globemaster II was used extensively, carrying supplies and troops between Japan and South Korea. The helicopter appeared in its first major conflict, as it rapidly transported troops over terrain that was almost impassable to ground vehicles. An operation involving twelve Sikorsky S-55 helicopters moved a battalion of 1,000 marines more than 16 miles in four hours. Famously, the Bell Model 47 (known as the H-13 Sioux in the U.S. Army) helped to save many lives, as it carried wounded troops from the battlefield to the Mobile Army Surgical Hospital (MASH) units. Helicopters also took part in air-sea rescues of pilots downed in the sea.

Cold War

DURING THE SO-CALLED 'COLD War' period, both sides produced many new aircraft as each strove to maintain supremacy in the air. In the early years of the period the focus was on the fighters, as the West progressed from the F-86 Sabre to the F-100 Super Sabre,

and the Soviets advanced from the MiG-15 to the MiG-19. New shapes took to the skies as nations vied with each other to produce faster aircraft with greater altitude capabilities, and increased firepower. One significant new design, the Convair F-102A Delta Dagger became the world's first delta-winged combat aircraft, the first super-sonic all-weather interceptor, and the first fighter without guns. It was designed to intercept Russian bombers in polar airspace en-route to America. Electronic equipment on board the F-102 would locate the enemy aircraft, the F-102's on-board radar would guide it into position, and the electronic fire control system would automatically fire its air-to-air rockets and missiles.

The Russians also adopted the delta-wing concept, around the same period, in the Mig-21 Fishbed that first flew in 1955. It became the most numerous jet fighter aircraft in the world, with over 8,000 built, and served with more than 40 countries. A simple, short-range day fighter when built, it was updated with more powerful engine, avionics and weaponry, and served with distinction in Vietnam against the American-built

ABOVE
B-52 bomber taking off from RAF Fairford
BELOW
Hawker Hunter

McDonnell-Douglas Phantom II, which was one of the most versatile fighter-bombers of that time. The French also utilised the delta-shaped wing in the Dassault Mirage III fighter, probably the best French military aircraft of all time, as testified by orders from fifteen air forces.

The use of electronics in air warfare, and associated countermeasures, came to prominence during the Vietnam War. Dedicated electronic warfare aircraft took part in 'Wild Weasel' operations to seek out, and destroy, enemy ground radar and missile positions. Best known of these were the

McDonnell-Douglas F4G Phantom, and the Republic F-105G Thunderchief with its radar jamming systems and Shrike anti-radar missiles.

Defence of the UK airspace, from incursions by Russian bombers and reconnaissance aircraft, was carried out initially by the Hawker Hunter fighter, by day, and the all-weather Gloster Javelin fighter. These were later replaced by the English Electric Lightning twin-engine interceptor that was itself superseded by the Panavia Tornado F3, an air defence variant of the multi-role combat aircraft produced by a consortium of manufacturers from Britain, Germany and Italy. The Tornado fea-

BELOW
Avro Vulcan V-bomber
of the RAF

tured the variable geometry 'swing wing' concept that provided excellent flight characteristics over a wide speed-range, a principle also used by the Americans in the General Dynamics F-111 bomber, and the Russians in the Tupolev T-22M Backfire bomber.

The Boeing B-52 Stratofortress first went to war in 1965, in Vietnam, where it carried out bombing raids from bases as far away as Guam in the Pacific. Even after the Cold War ended in 1991, the B-52 remained in service and, during the Gulf War in 1991, delivered forty percent of all munitions dropped on Iraq by the United States and its allies. It is predicted that the B-52 could be flying for the U.S. Air Force into the year 2045, almost a century after its development began. In Britain, offensive capability had progressed with the introduction of the Canberra medium-bomber, and the Vickers Valiant heavy bomber. The Handley Page Victor, later an in-flight refuelling tanker, had crescent-shaped wings so designed to maintain a constant critical Mach number from root to wingtip. Avro's Vulcan delta-wing aircraft, the third of the famous trio of 'V-Bombers', remained in service for more than thirty years.

Russian bombers of the era included the Myasishchev 'Bison', and the turbo-propeller powered Tupolev Tu-95 'Bear'.

Vertical Take-off and Landing

WHILE THE BALLOON, HELICOPter, and airship were all capable of 'vertical take-off and landing', the concept had received little consideration for use in heavier-than-air, fixed-wing aircraft. In battlefield situations, where conventional airfields were either non-existent or impractical, such aircraft could be valuable in the close-support role, or for carrying out combat air patrols, while operating from small forest clearings, desert strips, and roads. Various means of achieving vertical flight were tried, including the Convair XFY-1 'Pogo' that first flew in 1954, and earned itself the distinction of being the first successful 'vertical take-off and

BELOW Convair XFY-1 Pogo before take-off. The Pogo was an attempt to devise a practical vertical take-off and landing (VTOL) combat aircraft

landing' fixed-wing aircraft in the history of aviation. The turbo-propeller powered 'Pogo' was similar in appearance to most conventional aircraft except for its cruciform tail, fitted with wheels, on which it took off and landed: it never entered service. The later, jet-engine powered Ryan X-13 Vertijet used a form of thrust vectoring, but needed a vertical platform for take-off and landing, thus rendering it somewhat inflexible in operation. The British Aerospace Harrier first flew operationally in 1969, becoming the world's first vertical take-off and landing, fixed-wing aircraft to enter service. The Harrier achieves transition between conventional and vertical flight through moveable nozzles that direct engine thrust downward, during take-off and landing, and rearward for forward flight.

Spy Planes and Stealth Aircraft

THE LOCKHEED U-2 'DRAGON Lady' is a single-seat, single-engine aircraft, operated initially by the Central Intelligence Agency (CIA), later by the United States Air Force, and can fly at altitudes in excess of 70,000 feet. Officially a 'Utility' aircraft, hence its designation letter 'U', in reality it is an intelligence gathering aircraft, or 'spy plane', using a range of electronic and optical instruments to gather information. The U-2 first flew over Russia in 1956 and, for five years, its cameras took photos of ICBM missile testing sites and military installations. On May 1st 1960, a U-2 piloted by Francis Gary Powers was shot down over the Soviet Union, and Powers was sent to prison.

A radical new concept took to the skies in 1981 with the first flight of a so-called 'stealth' fighter. Actually, a tactical strike aircraft, the Lockheed F-117 Nighthawk was specifically designed to minimise its visibility to enemy radar by a combination of its shape, which had multiple reflecting flat surfaces to scatter radar returns, and its special coating of radar absorbing material. The F-117A first saw action in December 1989, during Operation Just Cause in Panama, but first came to prominence when, in the Gulf War of the early 1990s, it was the only coalition jet allowed to strike targets inside Baghdad's city limits. Using laser-guided bombs it attacked military targets and power stations, and flew more than a third of the bombing missions on the first day of the war.

Stealth is not the preserve of the fighter. The Northrop Grumman B-2 Spirit multi-role bomber is capable of delivering both conventional and nuclear munitions. A combination of 'stealthy' design features, including reduced acoustic, infrared, electromagnetic, and radar signatures, all coupled with its long range and large bomb capacity, give it many of the attributes required in an effective, modern bomber.

Chapter 12

Supersonic Passenger Flight and Beyond

ABOVE
Charles Yeager, the first man to exceed the speed of sound, in the cockpit of Air Force Bell XS-I

BELOW Captain Charles 'Chuck' Yeager (left), Major G Lundquist and Captain J Fitzger pictured in front of 'Glamorous Glennis'

"We'll go into orbit. We'll go to the moon. This business has no limits."
— **Richard Branson, 2005**

THE FIRST PILOT TO EXCEED THE speed of sound, and return to a safe landing, was U.S. Air Force Captain Charles E. (Chuck) Yeager, while flying the Bell XS-1, Number 46-062, on October 14th 1947. Launched from the modified bomb-bay of a B-29, the rocket-powered experimental aircraft named 'Glamorous Glennis' flew over the dry lakebeds in the Mojave Desert in California, and landed at the Muroc Test Centre (later to become Edwards Air Base). The fact that Mach 1, the technical term for the speed of sound, had been exceeded was declared 'Top Secret', and was not acknowledged until reports were leaked to the press several months later.

Technology derived from man's achievement of supersonic flight was used to develop military aircraft that were faster than the early pioneers of flight could have imagined. Unofficially nicknamed 'Blackbird,' the Lockheed SR-71 was developed as a long-range, strategic reconnaissance aircraft, capable of flying at speeds over Mach 3.2, and at 85,000 feet. It set a new, world speed record when it flew between New York and London in 1 hour 54 minutes and 56.4 seconds, on September 1st 1974, at an average speed of 1,806.964 miles per hour. Supersonic technology was also applied in the world of civil aviation.

Concorde

IN 1961, THE BRITISH AIRCRAFT Corporation (BAC) and the French company Sud-Aviation each submitted proposals for long-range, and medium-

ABOVE Lockheed SR-71 Blackbird reconnaissance aircraft

range, supersonic passenger aircraft. Direct consultations between the British and French governments had taken place on the subject of the supersonic airliner, but the two companies' individual design concepts failed to satisfy their respective governments' wish for joint working. By the time of the Farnborough Air Show in September 1962, agreement was so close that a model of the proposed aircraft was shown on the BAC stand. This attracted much Press and public attention, and there was some speculation that the expected Anglo-French agreement to build a SST (supersonic transport) might be announced.

The following month four men, each an aeronautical engineer of international repute, were closeted for one day in an office in Paris. With a single draughtsman and drawing board, they were instructed to finalise a common three-view layout for medium- and long-range versions of the SST. From Britain were Dr A. E. (later Sir Archibald) Russell, technical director of BAC's Filton Division, and Dr W. J. Strang, his chief engineer. From Sud-Aviation, Pierre Satre and Lucien Servanty, technical director and chief engineer respectively, represented the French. These men produced the design layout for the aircraft that was later known as 'Concorde', its name reflecting the joint working relationship between the two nations. There was, however, a difference of opinion over the name: the British preferred the Anglicised spelling 'Concord', but later relented. At the rollout ceremony of the first aircraft at

BELOW Concorde taking-off from London Heathrow

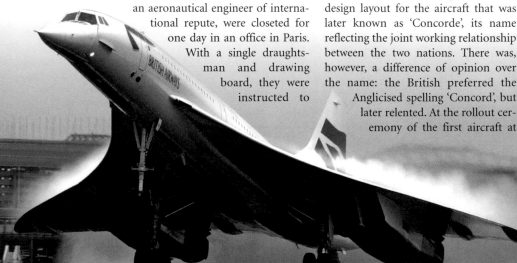

ABOVE
Concorde waiting for clearance on the runway, displaying its elegant lines

Toulouse in December 1967, Mr Anthony Wedgwood Benn, the British Minister of Technology, said that the British 'Concord' should, from now on, also be written with an 'e'.

By mid-1967, 16 airlines had taken a total of 74 Concorde options, albeit for a larger capacity version that was subsequently shelved. A decision was made to proceed with production of the smaller, interim prototype version. First flown in March 1969, authority was given for nine Concorde airframes to be built: two prototypes, two pre-production development aircraft, two ground test airframes, and three production aircraft. All versions were to be powered by four Rolls-Royce/Snecma Olympus 593 engines. Two production lines were established, one in Filton, Bristol, and

one in Toulouse, France. The two manufacturers were each responsible for manufacture of different sub-assemblies and smaller parts of the aircraft, these being transported between the two sites for final assembly. Inevitably, this method added to the substantial costs already incurred in the design and development of the project.

BOAC (later to become British Airways) and Air France signed contracts for a total of nine Concordes in July 1972. All of the prospective overseas airline customers, including Pan American and TWA, cancelled their options. These cancellations effectively signalled the end for Concorde, as a profitable commercial enterprise, even before it had flown in airline service. Eventually, in December 1973, the first production Concorde took

THE LITTLE BOOK OF FLIGHT | **119**

Airport, Washington. On November 22nd 1977, after a long delay due to protests over noise concerns in the vicinity of Kennedy Airport in New York, British Airways and Air France began supersonic services to New York from London and Paris, respectively. Supersonic flight between Europe and America made the world of the more affluent traveller a much smaller place. Those who could afford the considerable expense of the fare could travel between the continents, for business or other purposes, and return on the same

to the air. A period of extensive route proving trials followed, before entry into airline service.

British Airways began scheduled operations of its Concorde fleet with a London-Bahrain service, and Air France with a Paris-Rio service, via Dakar, on January 21st 1976. Transatlantic services to Washington DC, from both London and Paris, began on May 24th 1976, with two Concordes, one each from British Airways and Air France, landing simultaneously, at Dulles

day. In a remarkable demonstration of the possibilities in supersonic passenger flight, Richard Noble, the British world land speed record holder, set a new record by crossing the Atlantic three times in one day, aboard Concorde, on November 22nd 1987.

On July 25th 2000, tragedy struck when Air France Concorde F-BTSC crashed near Paris: debris on the runway caused a tyre to burst on take-off, and ruptured a fuel tank causing a serious fire, and reduced engine power. The loss of 109 people on board, and four on the ground, led to the aircraft being grounded for extensive modifications. Although it re-entered service in 2001, its future was anything but secure. Although more than 2.5 million passengers have flown supersonically in the British Airways Concorde fleet, the era of the supersonic passenger airliner ended when, on 24th October 2003, three British Airways Concorde aircraft landed at Heathrow Airport, shortly after 4pm. Concorde had made its last commercial flight after 27 years in operation.

BELOW
The final touch down for Concorde, 24th October 2003

Concordski

ON DECEMBER 31ST 1968 THE PRO-totype of the first supersonic airliner to fly, the Tupolev Tu-144, took off on its maiden flight from Zhukovski, USSR. Due to its resemblance to Concorde it was nicknamed 'Concordski', or some-times 'Konkordski', by the West. It was, in fact, significantly different in its wing shape but apart from its canard 'fore-plane' control surfaces was otherwise similar in layout to Concorde. It was claimed that much of the Tu-144 design

resulted from industrial espionage, hence the many similarities. After the horrific crash of the Tupolev Tu-144 at the Paris Air Show in 1973, many doubted that the Tu-144 would be little more than a symbol of Iron Curtain technology.

After several years of development, the Tu-144 commenced scheduled serv-ice on the route between Moscow and Alma-Ata, initially carrying only mail and freight. A total of 55 passenger flights were made, starting in November 1977, and the last on June 1st 1978, some seven months later, when the flights were discontinued after another crash. Aeroflot, the Russian airline, continued to fly the Tu-144 on freight and mail services after the official end of service, with some additional non-scheduled flights through the 1980s, including a flight from the Crimea to Kiev in 1987. A total of 102 scheduled flights were made in Aeroflot service.

In 1990, Tupolev approached NASA and offered a Tu-144 as a test bed for the NASA High Speed Commercial Research program, that was intended to develop the design for a second-generation supersonic jetliner. In 1995, a Tu-144D that was built in 1981 but with only 82 hours and 40 minutes total flight time, was taken out of storage and, after extensive modification at a total cost of $350 million, was re-designated the Tu-144LL. It made a total of 27 flights in 1996 and 1997 before the project was cancelled in 1999.

The Auto and Technik Museum in Sinsheim, Southern Germany has both a Tu-144 and a retired Air France Concorde on display, the only place in the world showing both aircraft.

Boeing SST

IN 1962, THE NATIONAL AERO-nautics and Space Administration (NASA) began the SCAT (Supersonic Commercial Air Transport) program in America. On June 5th 1963, President John F. Kennedy announced that such a program was authorised, shortly followed by the Federal Aviation Authority (FAA) request for proposals for a supersonic transport design. Three airframe constructors, and three engine manufacturers, were each asked to submit their designs by the following January.

Boeing had been working on a concept for SST aircraft since 1952, as part of their corporate philosophy for future developments. By 1960, the company was spending in excess of $1million, annually, on this project. Although the delta-wing layout was favoured by some of the designers, the variable-sweep wing alternative emerged as the favoured design for a 150-seat aircraft that would be capable of non-stop, supersonic flight across the Atlantic. In 1966, after requests from the FAA for a larger 250-seat aircraft, the Boeing variable-sweep wing, 277-seat aircraft won

LEFT Air France Concorde F-BVFB is placed beside a Russian Tupolev 144 on the roof of the Museum of Transport in Sinsheim, Germany, the only place showing both examples of a supersonic airliner

the contract from the competing Lockheed L-2000 double-delta wing proposal. One of the benefits of variable geometry gives an aircraft the ability to take off and land at lower speeds, and in less distance, than would a comparable fixed wing aircraft. However, there is a disadvantage in that the variable-sweep option is more complicated to design, manufacture, and maintain.

Boeing had predicted that, if the design and construction of prototypes were to begin in early 1967, the first flight could be made in early 1970. Production aircraft manufacture could begin in early 1969, with flight testing in late 1972: the first aircraft could then be certificated, and introduced to airline service in mid-1974. Boeing

claimed that, by 1980, there would be a market for a larger SST, with a total of between 700 and 1,000 aircraft being required. Ambitious from the outset, the program was doomed to failure. The variable-sweep concept was abandoned in 1968, the seating requirement reduced to 234 seats, and the wing layout radically altered to a gull-wing shape. Two prototypes were begun in September 1969 but, amid a wave of protest against Concorde, the US Senate closed down the SST program completely on March 24th 1971.

BELOW
A B-52B launch aircraft lifts off with NASA's X-43A hypersonic research aircraft and its modified Pegasus booster rocket attached under its right wing

The Future

THE NASA X-43A, OR HYPER-X, research aircraft set a new, world speed record for a jet-powered aircraft when it achieved a velocity of Mach 9.6, or nearly 7,000 miles per hour on its third and final flight on November 16th 2004. Launched from its B-52 mother ship, the unmanned craft was boosted by a rocket-powered launch stage and then, after separation, achieved the record speed under the power of its supersonic ramjet, called 'Scramjet', engine. There are no plans for a manned aircraft capable of such speed in the foreseeable future.

While the sub-sonic, passenger-carrying airliner will be around for some years into the future, the likelihood for commercial passengers to once again experience the timesaving benefit of supersonic flight is less realistic. Environmental and sociological considerations will severely limit the number of routes that the supersonic airliner could fly, thus making such an aircraft uneconomic to develop and operate.

The Wright Brothers were first to design and build a heavier than-air flying craft that could be controlled while in the air. Every successful aircraft built since the 1902 Wright glider has had controls with which to roll either to the right or left, pitch up or down, and yaw from side to side. These basic control movements allow a pilot to manoeuvre an aircraft about all three axes, making it possible to fly from place to place. The evolution of the flying machine is not yet complete. We can only guess at how the ingenuity of mankind will overcome the challenges to be faced in the future of flight.

ABOVE
The Hyper-X prepares to launch from the B-52, prior to the world record attempt, 2004

Also available by the same author:

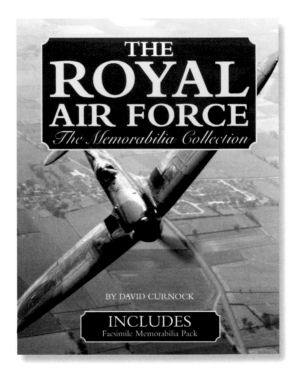

Available from all major stockists or online at:
www.greenumbrellashop.co.uk

The pictures in this book were provided courtesy of the following:

GETTY IMAGES
101 Bayham Street, London NW1 0AG

CODY IMAGES
www.codyimages.com

Book design and artwork by Kevin Gardner

Published by Green Umbrella Publishing

Publishers Jules Gammond and Vanessa Gardner

Compiled and written by David Curnock

The author would like to thank the proprietors of the following websites
for their valuable information and assistance:

*www.flyingmachines.org, www.centennialofflight.gov, www.enae.umd.edu www.ueet.nasa.gov,
www.history-of-flight.net, www.curtisswright.com, firstflight open.ac.uk, www.skygod.com,
www.sciencemuseum.org.uk, www.timetableimages.com*

BIBLIOGRAPHY

Jane's All the World's Aircraft – Harper Collins
The Illustrated Encyclopaedia of Major Aircraft of World War II – Francis K. Mason
World Air Power Journal – Aerospace Publishing Ltd